UP FOR DEBATE!

EXPLORING MATH THROUGH ARGUMENT

CHRIS LUZNIAK

Routledge
Taylor & Francis Group

NEW YORK AND LONDON

A Stenhouse Book

First published 2020 by Stenhouse Publishers

Published in 2024 by Routledge
605 Third Avenue, New York, NY 10017
4 Park Square, Milton Park, Abingdon, Oxon OX14 4RN

*Routledge is an imprint of the Taylor & Francis Group,
an informa business*

Cataloging-in-Publication data on file with the Library of Congress

Book design by Blue (www.bluedes.com)

ISBN: 978-1-62531-281-5 (pbk)
ISBN: 978-1-03-268296-9 (ebk)

To Ed + Pat,
the humans I hope to live up to someday.

CONTENTS

athematics, at its core, involves figuring out what is true. As philosopher of science Imre Lakatos described in his famous book Proofs and Refutations, argument is in fact how mathematics gets made.

Despite argument's centrality in the discipline, students get little exposure to thinking about mathematical issues from different perspectives. Typically, mathematics gets taught as pre-fabricated conclusions passed on from ancient peoples, with little room for students' ideas, curiosities, or questions. Not only does this common presentation do a disservice to students as learners, it provides a distorted view about the essence of mathematical thinking. Teaching math without argumentation is akin to teaching literature without creative writing or teaching soccer only through drills. Argumentation brings out the beauty of mathematics. It is the Big Game, where ideas come alive, where our understandings come out to play and get stretched to their limit.

You may be thinking, argumentation may be important; but, given all the curriculum teachers are responsible for, how can they possibly incorporate one more thing without adding a burdensome amount of planning to their precious preparation time?? Luckily, Chris Luzniak has an answer: introduce math debates. In this clearly written and well-detailed volume, he offers tools to bring authentic mathematical argumentation into classrooms through numerous math debate structures that will help students learn to use their mathematical voices. Whether through brief soap box debates to get ideas flowing or more extended debates that allow students to deeply engage with complex issues, Chris provides numerous tried and true examples, refined in his classroom as well as those of his colleagues, that work across content areas and grade levels.

The learning benefits of math debates will make it worth your time. Decades of research in mathematics education, captured in documents like National Council of Teachers of Mathematics Principles and Standards (2000), has shown the importance of so many things that math debates support. For instance, by having students present different ideas about problems, debates let students know that mistakes are okay, as is changing your mind. By focusing in on one concept at a time, debates provide students the chance to really make sense of ideas. By emphasizing verbal argumentation, debates give students opportunities to use math vocabulary in relationship to things in the world. The interpretive format of debatable questions—such as, which is hardest? which is best? where is the mistake? —foster students' metacognitive skills.

Importantly, these math debates structures do not only emphasize the talk students produce through talking routines; they also emphasize the sense students make of other people's ideas through listening routines. Too often, students go through math class thinking their main job is to produce correct answers. In other parts of life, however, success is not just about what we say but also how we respond to—and build on—what others say. Listening skills, considering other perspectives, and changing your mind graciously all help students to be more than just better math students. These skills help them to be better friends, classmates, and citizens.

So, what are you waiting for? It's time to #DebateMath!

ACKNOWLEDGMENTS

This book is made possible by the outpouring of love from so many wonderful humans I have encountered. Just as Newton claimed to have stood on the shoulders of giants, I write this standing alongside a community full of love.

I could not imagine ever writing this book without the support, encouragement, and love that exudes from Tracy Zager!! She took the time to notice me and encourage me. It is her kindness that led me to consider this endeavor. As an editor, she made it possible for one awkward math teacher to put practices into writing. She has been my mentor and my friend throughout this whole process, and I am forever indebted to her for all she has taught me. I am also appreciative of the love from the rest of the amazing team at Stenhouse. Amanda Bondi has guided the manuscript through many phases with care and attention. Thanks to Shannon for your help with so many details! Thanks to Nate for making a difficult situation look simple and smooth. Thanks to Tom, Jay, and everyone at Stenhouse for making this book shine. Most important, thank you to the exclamation point: for helping me convey my message, my energy, and giving Tracy extra work each round of edits!

I am forever grateful to my current school, the Archer School for Girls, for offering nothing but love and encouragement throughout this process. I am enamored by my brilliant, caring, and courageous colleagues, especially the supportive leadership: Elizabeth English, Karen Pavliscak, and Gretchen Warner. Caitlin Duffy started this journey with me and has been my friend and sounding board. Jemma Kennedy continued that journey after her and has been my personal mentor and thought partner. I am regularly amazed by these two strong female mathematicians. May these two and the entire Archer Math Department continue to be a constant source of inspiration. Everyone at Archer (not just the math teachers!) makes the complex job of teaching and learning something to look forward to each day. You make this career an act of love.

My love for teaching truly began in New York City, under the mentorship of Math for America and my first cooperating teacher, Erica Litke. In my early years of teaching, the reassurance from Erica and the leaders at Math for America kept me going. They helped me find my first job, and I am thankful for the friendship and collaboration of those first amazing colleagues, including Eyal Wallenberg, Melanie Smith, Megan Sciammarella, and Judith Steinhart. The thoughtfulness and gusto of my colleagues in New York City helped me to stay motivated and to grow as both a math teacher and a debate coach. Throughout my career in NYC, Math for America continued to be a community of love and support. Wonderful Math for America teachers from other schools, including Steve Viola and Michael Holmes, helped me explore and expand these debate ideas, and I am forever grateful to the leadership of director Kara Stern, whose encouragement helped me to believe in myself.

Listening is an act of love, and I am lucky to have marvelous friends who allow me to think out loud, who hear what I have to say, and who sometimes allow me to send them drafts to read! I am thankful for the love of Derek, Bill, Lauren, Josh, Timmy, Ogi, Joe, Jacob, Ali, Jaclyn, Rachel, Sarah, and Richard. Every little act of love does not go unnoticed. Answering a text at midnight can change my world. I am especially grateful of the love and support of my friend and partner, Peter Drocton. He has been there to support and encourage me when times were challenging.

My former Speech and Debate students in New York—*all* of them—showed unconditional love for me, their teammates, and the art of forensics. Thank you especially to Iselda, DeAndre, Brenda, Jamel, Bria, Ariel, Jaimie, Keianna, Andreina, Krystal, Kyle, Yennifer, and the countless other students who bravely spent their afternoons practicing and their weekends competing in tournaments. Each of these students exhibited the power of debate and inspired so much of what is in this book. I learned more from coaching these students than from competing as a student. These students are powerful beyond measure. I am also appreciative of the many adults who volunteered their time to help these students practice and grow, including Justin Welch, Robert Roberg, Jonathan Cerio, and Rick Raven. The art of debate and the National Speech & Debate Association are invaluable to education and our society.

As I tried to grow in my practice, hundreds of teachers online have openly shared ideas, collaborated on musings, and reached out in support countless times. The Math-Twitter-Blog-o-Sphere (#MTBoS) is a loving community of teachers around the globe willing to support one another through the ups and downs of this career. They are the dream math department. Ilana Horn has been this teacher's teacher many times over. Her love and guidance have taught me so much, and I am so grateful to her for taking the time to be a part of this book. Elizabeth Statmore has been my teaching soul mate. Julie Reulbach has been my cheerleader, reminding us all that we are not imposters. Casey McCormick has been my conference wife and reflection partner. Mary Bourassa continues to be such a lovely source of inspiration (and we are thankful for the resources she provides on wodb.ca). John Stevens inspires and awes me every time he speaks (and I'm grateful that his work could be included in this book!). Robert Kaplinsky has been my friend, my mentor, and my writing partner throughout the life of this book and an invaluable source of knowledge. Nanette inspires me (all of us really) to believe in myself with her enthusiasm. Fawn, Debbie, Lisa, Sara, Peg, Chrissy, Jonathan, Tina, Ashli, Howie, and countless other amazing math teachers have been my friends, mentors, and heroes. May I never stop learning from all of these wonderful humans.

Through the MTBoS, I have been able to share these debate ideas with teachers all around the country, and I am grateful for the early adopters who took a chance on me. The courage and perseverance of Karla Doyle, Patricia Vandenberg, and Claire Verti cannot be understated. They lovingly jumped into debating in math class and have boldly shared their experiences online. Teachers like these three inspire me regularly.

I owe so much of who I am to my MTBoS partners-in-pedagogy (and musical theater): Sam Shah and Mattie Baker. They have kept me focused and kept me honest. They have taught me how to be vulnerable. They have shared their love of teaching with me and with many teachers over the years. They have been selfless and supportive friends, rainbows on a gloomy day, and a boundless source of inspiration, encouragement, and love.

My love of math started in high school calculus with Nancy Barile. The passion with which she taught math sparked an interest that I did not understand at the time. Her English teacher counterpart, Carrie Cofer, drew me into the Speech and Debate world, and I am thankful that she never let me leave it. In college, my math interests only grew under the calm teaching and advising of Dr. Richard Little. These three teachers and mentors, now friends, set in motion a lifelong interest in and love for both math and debate. I can never repay them for all they have given me. Their teaching was truly an act of love.

Last, I could not be who I am today without the constant love and support of my family. My siblings—Dan and Kate—keep sending love to their ridiculous older brother. They have been a source of support in a difficult year. Most important, my parents have never wavered in their love and support. They worked hard to create possibilities for their children. My experiences, my career, and this book (!) are the result of all those countless years of love and support. This book is the result of those weekends you drove me to speech tournaments. Thank you to my family for the laughs, the hugs, and the notes of love.

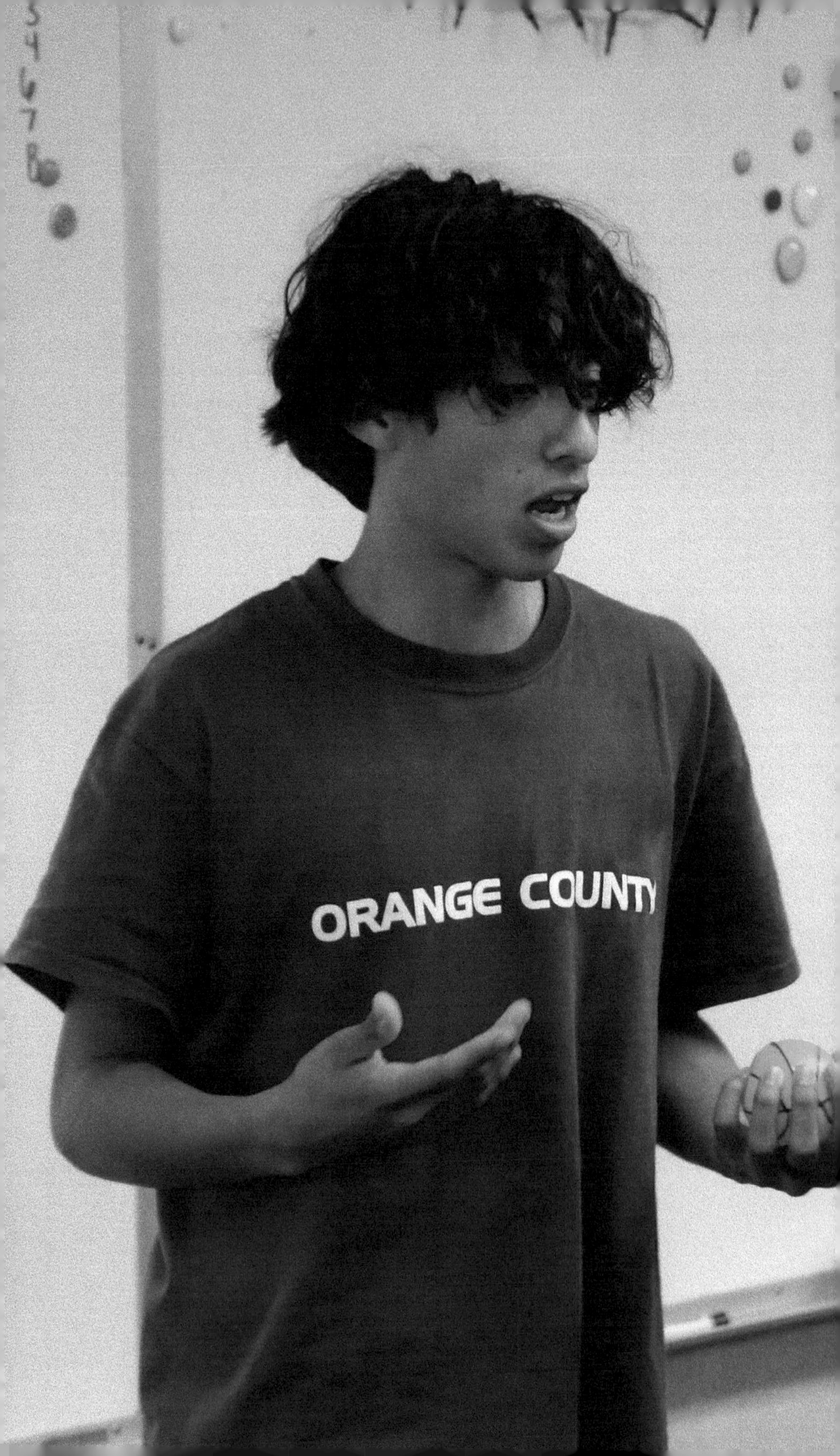
ORANGE COUNTY

CHAPTER 1

OPENING ARGUMENTS

I t is late September in Brooklyn, and our high school students are just starting to settle into their classes. Walking down the generic-public-school tiled-hallway, lined with light blue lockers, you turn into my math classroom, where algebra class is about to start. The space is crowded, and racially, ethnically, and linguistically diverse students take up nearly every seat in the room. On the board you see:

PREPARE AN ARGUMENT FOR THE STATEMENT:

_____ is the best method for solving the system

$$y = 2x$$
$$y = x + 1$$

Some of the students are thinking silently, others are writing some ideas down in their notebooks, and still others are whispering quietly with neighbors at their table groups. After a minute of think time, I pull the class together, and we start. I call on a student who has her hand in the air. She stands up to begin the debate, and I sit down. All eyes turn toward the standing student.

Izelda: *I claim that elimination is the best method for solving the system, and my warrant is because the variables are already stacked up, x on x. It's easy. Subtract.*

Hands go up in the air, and as she sits down, Izelda calls on the next student, who rises and says:

Jamal: *I hear that Izelda wants to use elimination, but I claim that substitution is the best method. Yeah, and my warrant is that both equations are already in y-equals. You just plug that stuff in for y. It's easy to solve from there.*

Before he sits down, Jamal points to Brinda, who stands. The class and I turn our eyes and knees to Brinda and listen:

Brinda: *Jamal said he wants substitution, but I concur with Izelda. I claim that elimination is the best method for solving the system and my warrant is that the steps to solve x are quick. You just get 0 equals x minus 1, which means x has to be 1. I can do it in my head.*

With no more hands in the air, Brinda sits. After a quiet moment, I ask the class if there are any further arguments. A shy student in the back raises his hand and stands to add:

Andre: *I claim . . . graphing is the best for solving, because both equations are easy to graph. They are already in* mx plus b *form, and I like when I can see it.*

I thank the students for their input, and then I instruct the class that, with these arguments in mind, they need to solve a *new* system of equations using what they think is the best method. The class jumps to action! I am excited to hear students starting another round of debate with their partners, and I notice they seem to feel less pressure debating with their partner than in front of the whole group, at least this early in the year.

■　　　■　　　■　　　■　　　■

Let's look at another example, with slightly older students:

A few periods later, just after lunch, my Algebra 2 class walks in and students see the following on the board:

THE BEST MISTAKE IS:

1) $3\sqrt{44b^9c}$

$3\sqrt{4}\sqrt{11}\sqrt{b^9}\sqrt{c}$

$3 \cdot 2\sqrt{11} \cdot b^3\sqrt{c}$

$6b^3\sqrt{11c}$

2) $\sqrt{200x^3y^8}$

$\sqrt{2}\sqrt{100}\sqrt{x^2}\sqrt{x}\sqrt{y^2}\sqrt{y^2}\sqrt{y^2}\sqrt{y^2}$

$\sqrt{2} \cdot \sqrt{10x}\sqrt{xyyyy}$

$xy^4\sqrt{20x}$

Students start discussing the mathematics with their partners at tables. I float around the room, listening to the student-to-student conversations. Then, after only about ninety seconds of discussion, I pull a student's name randomly from my deck of index cards (my "Cards of Math Destiny") and call on him. He rises to speak, and I sit down. The class turns to face the speaker.

> Matthew: *I claim the second one is the best mistake because I keep making the same one! I also forget to take the root off after I square root, like they did with the 100. It should have a 10, not a root 10 in the middle there.*

Matthew calls on Sammi to speak next. Matthew takes a seat as Sammi rises to begin her argument. The class shuffles in their seats to focus on Sammi.

> Sammi: *I see the mistake in number two, but I claim that number one has the best mistake and my warrant is that they made the mistake of square-rooting the power, which could make sense if you don't remember the rule. Or that square root is a one-half power.*

Students naturally start muttering to their partners, engaged in mathematical conversation inspired by the two brief ideas that were shared. I listen in for a moment and hear that students had a harder time finding the mistake in the first problem and need more time to think it through. I pause the debate there, and I ask students to explain the *correction* they would make in the first problem to their partner. Pencils in hands, students start re-solving the first problem, explaining their steps to their partners. I see some students writing

$\left(b^9\right)^{\frac{1}{2}}$ while other students are writing out $\sqrt{b}^2$ four times followed by a $\sqrt{b}$. The different approaches provide a quality discussion when students share out their approaches with the whole class a few minutes later.

. . . . .

Helping students find and use their voices is something teachers in all subjects strive for—we want students to build their understanding and confidence. However, the social and emotional risks often make it difficult for students to speak up, especially in math. As Dr. Ilana Horn explains in her book *Motivated*, "Students often avoid participating in mathematical discussions because publicly sharing their thinking is a socially risky endeavor" (2017, 3). Concerned with classroom status, many students fear making a mistake in front of their peers in math class. So, it can be difficult for many students to imagine sharing their thinking publicly. As a result, debates in math class must be facilitated thoughtfully and with care.

. . . . .

A different day, a different year, I'm no longer teaching in New York. I'm now on the West Coast, in an all-girls independent school. The location and the students have changed, but the math is still the same, and so is the debating.

Girls walk into our small calculus class and see Figure 1.1 on the board. It's early in the year, and we have been talking about how the slope of a graph relates to the velocity of an object. We have not begun talking about derivatives just yet. Using my random name caller (index cards), I call on students one at a time. They take turns, standing to debate their answers.

> **Casey:** *I claim Graph B does not belong because it is the only one that's continually increasing across the domain.*
>
> **Lizbeth:** *I claim that Graph D does not belong, and my reason is that it is the only graph where the person slows down, since the end is almost flat. The slope is 0 at the end.*
>
> **Julia:** *I claim it's Graph B that doesn't belong because it is the only one where the person is moving away from you the whole time.*
>
> **Traci:** *I claim Graph C doesn't belong because it is the only one with two x-intercepts.*

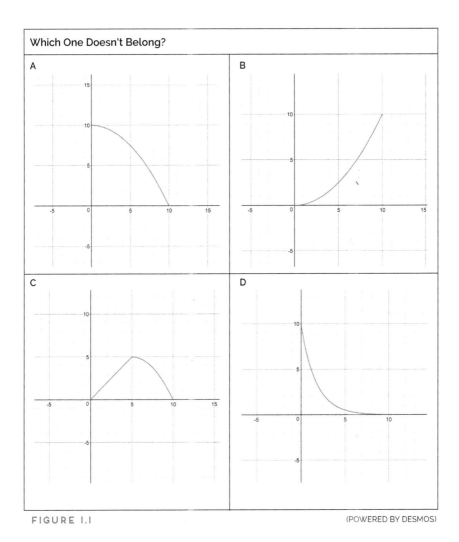

FIGURE I.I   (POWERED BY DESMOS)

Notice the use of math vocabulary in the students' responses. Additionally, though I did not specify that the graphs should be thought of as distance versus time graphs, two of the students are placing that context on the graphs to provide a way of interpreting them. This activity serves to both reinforce vocabulary as well as to formatively assess students' understandings of the current topic.

After two more students share out, I pause the conversation, as no student has discussed Graph A yet. I tell students to turn to a partner and come up with at least two arguments in favor of Graph A. The class jumps into discussion at their tables.

■   ■   ■   ■   ■

These examples are just the beginning! Now, imagine what can happen during the next thirty, fifty, or ninety minutes, after students have started the class with sense making, discussion, and oral arguments. Consider how much students are improving *one another's* math vocabulary and conceptual understanding by having these discussions. Think of how rich future classroom discussions can be because students know how to talk about mathematics together. Picture how well students can explain their processes to one another and consequently help their classmates understand mathematical ideas. Notice also the information the teacher gains in these moments. As students express and comment on their preferences and thinking, the instructor can gather formative assessment information.

I hope these classroom examples have you thinking about the possibilities for your classroom. These rich discussions may seem a bit out of reach at the moment, but in the following chapters, we'll explore how to work up to robust classroom debates, piece by piece. They are more attainable than you think, and the value of these classroom moments necessitates the effort. Yes, we teachers have a lot of expectations on our plates—from our schools, from our districts, and within ourselves—and yes, there is always the fear that students will act out or the class will become rowdy if we give them the opportunity to debate. However, we all want to inspire our students mathematically. We want to see each student's understanding and appreciation of math grow and flourish, along with their confidence. So, as teachers, we owe our students opportunities to develop their mathematical voices, craft their arguments, and engage in mathematical discussions. Debating math is a great way to provide those opportunities in class.

WHY I DEBATE IN MATH CLASS

Let me back up for a moment and explain why I believe so strongly in math debates. Years ago, during my first years as a secondary school math teacher in New York City public schools, I grew nostalgic for the high school Speech and Debate Team experiences I'd had as a student. I decided to start coaching debate, and I sought out a school in the area with a team I could help. The following year, I started my own Speech and Debate Team, which I spent the next seven years building and growing. Throughout both my student and coaching experiences, I saw the passion and engagement that debate instilled in the students on my team. Furthermore, in the subject of mathematics, a subject solidly grounded in reasoning, proof, and argumentation, I saw a place to connect debate strategies to content learning. So, I began trying to create a math classroom where students do the talking, explain their thinking, and critique one another's reasoning.

The potential for students' excitement was not the only factor that motivated me to bring debate into the math classroom. Much has been written about the positive effects of debate for students and classrooms. For example, debate has been shown to improve communication and critical thinking skills in general. "When students are encouraged to think aloud—specifically, when they practice critical skills with their peers—they gain experience they may then apply to their own internal reasoning processes" (Bellon 2000, 164).

The more I learned, the more I grew increasingly convinced that I had to find a way to bring debate into math class. I began visiting humanities classes to see what structures they had for debate, but nothing struck me as an authentic activity to adapt to my math class, an activity that would have students discussing while working on rich math content. Then, I found my inspiration in Boston. I stumbled upon a summer workshop on Debate Across the Curriculum, sponsored by the Boston Debate League. It was a workshop for teachers of all subjects, sharing some common structures for student debate. Although I did not use many of the activities exactly as presented in the session, I found the spark I needed—a spark that I have spent the past several years fanning into a set of rich tasks and activities for my math students. With fifteen years of teaching experience (so far!), I feel confident that I have embarked on a worthwhile journey with debate. I have taught math courses from seventh grade through calculus (and beyond), and I have found ways to incorporate debates into them all.

What I most enjoy is seeing debate work at a wide range of schools. I started debating math in an East Coast public school, where my overflowing classroom boasted a truly diverse population of students, both in backgrounds and in existing math proficiency. I loved how debate structures engaged all students, especially those students other teachers may have considered to be quieter students—students who were English language learners, students with significant learning differences, or students who generally had shier personalities. These same debate activities and routines worked just as well when I moved to the West Coast. Students in my all-girls independent school (just down the road from Hollywood) find developing mathematical arguments equally as engaging as did my students in New York City. Students continue to find their voices and jump into debates.

I believe debates have heightened all my students' abilities to discuss and explore with math and to construct understanding. I believe debates have increased engagement in my math classes, drawing all types of personalities (even those shy students) into *active* learning, and I believe debates have given a voice to all my math learners. For me, debating math is now a real and important part of the fabric of my classroom culture. I hope students learn that anyone can talk about and debate math and know that doing math can involve opinions and arguments. I delight in seeing students struggle as their mindset shifts from the idea that math is where you learn formulas and solve a worksheet of similar problems to the idea that math is a living subject, where people discuss and debate best strategies or interpretations of information. My experience teaching mathematics through debate is why I believe debates can make a huge difference in any math classroom.

And I am not the only teacher who has tested this out. I have shared my ideas through many professional development opportunities and math teacher conferences across the country. I started in New York City, working with Math for America to help both math and science teachers incorporate debate into their classes, and I continue to work with teachers of all levels of experience whenever I can. My favorite comment a teacher said after attending a session was: "The more students talk about something, the deeper their understanding." Debate has made a definite impact on the depth of understanding for students in dozens of middle and high school classrooms, and many of these teachers have shared their work online. Through these collaborative experiences, teachers have created a plethora of debate activities for their students, and you can too! This book can help you join in this community of teachers (who #DebateMath).

We teachers know that our students love to share their opinions—a huge part of adolescence and processing. So, why not harness that power by creating structured debate activities in the classroom?

WHY *YOU* SHOULD DEBATE IN MATH CLASS

Much has been published about the benefits and the need for classroom discourse and argumentation. In their book *Intentional Talk*, Elham Kazemi and Allison Hintz state: "Everything we know about student learning and classroom practice tells us that classroom conversations are crucial to mathematics learning" (2014, vii). Students need to discuss and debate their ideas to deepen their learning. Additionally, the Common Core State Standards of Mathematical Practice (SMP) emphasize constructing and critiquing arguments (#3), and *Principles to Actions* by the National Council of Teachers of Mathematics (NCTM) talks extensively about research supporting collaborative experiences and sense making: "Specifically, learners should have experiences that enable them to . . . construct knowledge socially, through discourse, activity, and interaction related to meaningful problems" (2014, 9). The authors of *Principles to Actions* go on to say, "Effective mathematics teaching engages students in discourse to advance the mathematical learning of the whole class . . . . The discourse in the mathematics classroom gives students opportunities to share ideas and clarify understandings, construct convincing arguments . . . develop a language for expressing mathematical ideas, and learn to see things from other perspectives" (29).

Reasoning and discourse are core tenets of effective teaching for both NCTM and the Common Core, and debate meets these needs. Through debate, we can create classrooms where all students can participate equally, and where all students have a voice in their learning (which is empowering *and* deepens students' learning). What's more, classroom discussions and debates set students up for success in future math and science classes and careers: "Students who learn to articulate and justify their own mathematical ideas, reason through their own and others' mathematical explanations, and provide a rationale for their answers develop a deep understanding that is critical to their future success in mathematics and related fields" (Carpenter, Franke, and Levi 2003, 6). Our innovation economy requires adults who know how to think and talk together, to listen to multiple perspectives, and to make solid arguments.

Thus, debate is crucial for a powerful mathematics classroom. In their book *Exploring Talk in School*, Neil Mercer and Steve Hodgkinson declare that classroom talk "is the most important educational tool for guiding the development of understanding and for jointly constructing knowledge." To have richer and more engaged classrooms, we need to create the space for discourse and debate. However, as Mercer and Hodgkinson point out, "Many children either don't know how to carry on a productive discussion, or don't realize that this is what they are expected to do by the teacher" (65). Teachers are often unsure how to facilitate quality discourse, and students are not aware of its importance. That is where this book can come to the rescue! We will explore strong routines and questions that safely promote student discourse in math class.

Let's improve our students' experiences in the math classroom and increase their engagement as young mathematicians by having students "construct viable arguments and critique the reasoning of others," as SMP3 instructs us (Common Core 2010). Let's make math class a rich and exciting place where students not only *do* math but also *discuss* math. Let's help students see the importance of verbalizing their ideas and justifying their conclusions. Let's create exciting and equitable classrooms that allow all students to grow and succeed. Let's make math class a place for debate!

BUILDING THE CASE—
GOALS FOR THE BOOK

Like any good lesson, we cannot begin our journey into debate without clear objectives.

First, and foremost, I want to bring debates "to life" for you in this book. Though this work normally takes place with teachers in person, I want to do my best to help you feel the experience of live debates while reading this book. We want to "see" what is possible. As you read through this book, try to imagine how these activities could fit into your class. Imagine some of your students as the ones quoted in the examples. If you want a more concrete visual, you can even watch videos of my classroom in action at luzniak.com/media. Feel free to check out the five-minute PBS video entitled "Encouraging Debate" right now—it will help you understand the power and the flow of math debates and see the possibilities for your classes right away.

PBS "ENCOURAGING DEBATE" VIDEO

My second goal for this book is to provide you with concrete structures and routines that will help you get your students talking and debating. We will explore several structures, working to find ones that fit *you* as the teacher you are with *your* students. More importantly, we will look into the *why* behind each structure. Our work will especially stress the brevity and practicality of debate structures, which make it possible for you to add these structures to your classroom right away, while teaching the content you are already focusing on. Additionally, we will see a sequence that I have developed and used to introduce these debate structures in class. We don't jump into full-scale debates in September. We start small, with quick warm-up routines, and then we build incrementally from there throughout the fall. Most of the information on this progression will be found in Chapters 2 and 4.

Third, we need to start writing solid debate-worthy questions for your class, immediately! We will explore quick and concrete ways (as well as some more complex ways) to change your existing math problems into more debatable ones. By increasing the debate-ability of your questions, you will unlock opportunities for debates and discussions to come alive in your classroom. This will be our work in Chapter 3.

Last, and perhaps most important, you will see examples and activities meant to inspire you. Many examples will be included throughout each chapter, and more examples are being shared online all the time (#DebateMath). We all teach different students, but in the end, students are students and humans are humans. Students can be engaged in inquisitive problem solving with thoughtful facilitation.

I hope this book makes you think and inspires you. Debate and mathematics have been my two passions for years, and I am excited to share my story—teacher to teacher—of how bringing the two together has transformed my math classes and can transform yours. Enjoy!

CHAPTER 2

MAKING THE CASE

E arly in my teaching career, I learned a lot about how to have productive conversations from my thoughtful colleagues. The faculty at my school in New York believed each student who acted inappropriately should have a mediated discussion with the teacher or student he or she offended as the first step in a process. I remember my first mediation with a student. Both the student and I were nervously seated at a table, facing each other. We were each instructed by our Dean of Students to speak about the incident from our own perspectives, using only *I* statements. For example, each of us discussed our side of the story with statements like "*I* heard . . ." or "*I* saw . . ." rather than "*You* . . ." Both of us were given sentence starters that framed how to discuss or respond in this mediated conversation, and they worked!

This shift from accusing others to describing our own points of view was a revelation to me back then, and I realized that scaffolding conversation through structures had clear classroom implications. If adults need to be taught how to have certain conversations, the same must be true for students. Perhaps some students do not speak in math class because they don't know how? Our students can have rich discussions, but sometimes they need clarity on what to say and how to say it. That's where the tools of debate come in.

DEVELOPING DEBATE

In my experience, the best way to begin introducing the tools of debate is through warm-up routines that take only two or three minutes of class time, at the outset. These activities can fit within your already existing plans, and the teachers I have worked with have found a lot of success starting small. When you are ready, you

can extend the process in many directions, developing everything from a larger debate activity for tomorrow's lesson to a full-scale debate as a performance assessment, which we will dig into in later chapters. At the beginning, however, turning one or two moments of a lesson into debatable moments is plenty and helps us fit debate nicely within our current plans. As one teacher shared, "The beauty of #DebateMath is that it doesn't actually require additional resources—it's easy to incorporate debate into the content and lessons we already teach."

What's more, these little changes can have a positive effect on the classroom culture and students' desires to argue and justify. The starting routines can quickly shift your classroom into a place where students are eager to discuss their ideas and respectfully critique one another's reasoning.

So, how do we do it? How do we get our students effectively debating in math class? There are two big pillars that form the foundation of all the debate routines we will explore in this book. These keys to making debatable moments in the classroom are:

1. Talking and listening routines for students
2. Debatable questions from the teacher

This chapter is all about the first requirement—Talking and Listening Routines. We will discuss writing debatable questions in Chapter 3.

TALKING ROUTINES

So how do we get students to talk with debate language? First, we must define an *argument*. An argument is a statement meant to convince or persuade. (Notice that the definition has nothing to do with yelling or screaming!) We can share this definition with students, but it is not something they need to remember. We want them to understand that an argument must be convincing, and that being the loudest or most dramatic person in the room is not what we mean by convincing. We want well-thought-out explanations.

What is most important for students to know as we develop our Talking Routines is that *every argument has two key parts*:

- The claim—the controversial statement or opinion being made.
- The warrant—the reason or justification for the claim.

These definitions lead us to the fundamental routine for students debating in class. They will use the sentence frame:

"My claim is _____,

and my warrant is _____."

I introduce this Talking Routine in the first days of school, and it is all we need to get started debating! It takes about two minutes to set up (we will get into the details of how in just a bit), and we rely on this routine of saying, "My claim is . . . , and my warrant is . . ." anytime we debate, all year long.

To stress the importance of this sentence starter and to make it easy to come back to, I have it posted on three (or some years all four) of the walls of my classroom (Figure 2.1). That way, no matter what direction a student is facing, they can always see the words. These visual reminders are a big help in the first few days as students slowly become familiar with the sentence frame. They are also a safety net anytime students are called on to speak because they provide a focal point if students do not want to look around the room at their classmates.

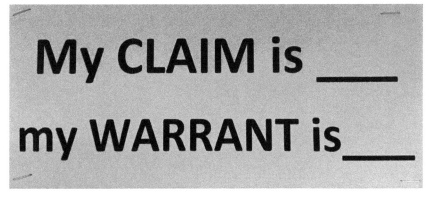

FIGURE 2.1

Let me take a moment here to further explain the terms *claim* and *warrant*. When we introduce these key words in class, we can give some examples to make the terms clear to all students. The *claim* is basically the person's opinion. A claim could be "cats are better than dogs" or "the death penalty should be abolished" or "solving by substitution is the easiest way to solve a system of equations." A claim is always controversial in the sense that there are always opposing sides. Even if all your students have the same opinion, a claim has the *potential* to have an opposing side. In other words, even if all your students think cats are better than dogs, one student could feasibly argue against that claim if necessary.

The word *warrant* is the one that students are less familiar with, but we can emphasize that warrant simply means the reason or explanation. Most students have only heard the term used by police in movies and television. Scenes of police saying they have a warrant to search a house or a warrant for a person's arrest are common, but even in these instances, the warrant is the reason. It is the reason to search or to make an arrest. Similarly, in debates, the warrant is the reason for your side of the argument. You cannot have a complete argument without sound reasoning. If you think dogs are better than cats, you have to say *why*. If you want to argue that solving systems of equations by substitution is the best method, you have to say *why*. So, the warrant is the justification or the reason *why*.

Putting these pieces together, some examples of student statements in claim and warrant form are:

- "My claim is dogs are better than cats, and my warrant is that dogs are soft and cuddly."
- "My claim is that $\frac{1}{3}$ is greater than $\frac{1}{2}$, and my warrant is that it has the larger denominator." (False, I know, but still a complete argument!)
- "My claim is parabola A is easier to sketch, and my warrant is that it is already in vertex form."
- "My claim is that the limit does not exist, and my warrant is that the right- and left-hand limits will be different numbers."

Claims and warrants are the student tools we need to create a debate culture in our classrooms. Once students have the language to engage in the debate, they can argue anything. Just as I was writing this chapter, I had an algebra class debate the best method for solving a system of equations.

The responses were:

WHAT IS THE BEST METHOD FOR SOLVING THIS SYSTEM OF EQUATIONS?

$$y = 5x - 6$$
$$y = 4x - 2$$

Sarah: *My claim is that substitution is best, and my warrant is because you can just plug in one equation. So, you could say* 5x minus 6 equals 4x minus 2, *and then you could solve it really easily.*

Jocylen: *My claim for the best is graphing. My warrant is because it is already set up in* mx plus b *form. So, all you have to do is plug in the numbers and graph it out.*

Raechel: *My claim is that the best method for solving this system of equations would be graphing. My warrant is that because it is already in* y equals mx plus b *form, it makes it easier to graph because you already have the y-intercept, and I'm good with graphing. Sometimes it takes a while, but it helps me see things clearer.*

Note that this healthy debate is calm and measured. Using the formal debate language of *claim* and *warrant* is a way to signal to students that our debates have a level of seriousness and decorum. Using the sentence starter holds students to a professional standard of debating in math class.

As we all know, helping students develop routines takes practice. For example, many teachers leave time for everyone to write the homework in their planner during the last few minutes of class, and they may explicitly repeat this routine daily for several weeks (or longer), making sure students hold to this expectation. Eventually, our students remember to add homework to their planner each day because it is an ingrained routine. Similarly, we want the Talking Routine of "My claim is . . . , and my warrant is . . ." to be just as ingrained in students. So, we need to make it an explicit routine anytime we have a debatable moment in class.

Because we want students to practice this Talking Routine, we also need to make sure to have a debate-worthy question (more on this in Chapter 3!) as a regular part of class. I like to have a debatable warm-up activity at least once or twice a week, especially in the first month of school. It is important for students to use the Talking Routine correctly and often.

To emphasize this point, in the first few weeks, when a student mistakenly says, "My claim is that dividing is the best first step *because* . . . ," we can kindly and quickly interrupt by reminding them to say, "and my warrant is . . ." instead of the word *because*. This can be done as subtly as possible, with the discussion still moving forward. However, we really want students to stick to the sentence frame we establish, and that requires the teacher to make some minor corrections the first few times a class debates. Enforcing precision early on can pay off a lot in the long run.

As a bonus, because I emphasize the two-part answer so much, students talk about how accustomed they become to explaining their answer in my class. My students say: "In Mr. Luzniak's class, every answer always has two parts." So, even when we are not explicitly having a debate in class, students still tend to explain or justify their answers due to the repetition of two-part answers in our debate activities. This has been an important shift in the classroom culture for many teachers I have worked with, and I hope it will be true for you too!

One final point I want to make about this Talking Routine is "the magic" of it. Students not only get in the habit of a two-part answer but also feel empowered by the formality of it. I see this phenomenon most in my quieter students, my shier students, and my English language learners. Using the words *claim* and *warrant*, which are not usually part of most students' day-to-day vernacular, creates an added safety net for all students to participate. Even though they are expressing an opinion, they are using formal language given by the teacher. So, it is almost as if the opinion is not theirs, or the opinion they are expressing is less personal. Students do not feel overly exposed when debating because the sentence starter helps lower the stakes for students, and it provides scaffolding that temporarily brackets their defense mechanisms. Students who normally do not feel comfortable talking to the whole class, those who pull me aside on the first day to tell me that talking in front of others makes them incredibly nervous, suddenly feel empowered when they use the sentence starter because it is less personal (somebody else's language) and brief (just one sentence).

Though I stick to the words *claim* and *warrant* every year, I want to encourage you to use whatever sentence frame you feel works best for you. It is not these two words in particular that are magic but rather the formality of them that works. Other words could be substituted for *claim* and *warrant* just as easily. For instance, I have worked with teachers who modify the Talking Routine to "My claim is . . . , and my justification is . . ." or "My statement is . . . , and my warrant is . . ." I have also worked with some science teachers who decided to make a more science-vocabulary version of this: "My hypothesis is . . . , and my evidence is . . ." There are many variations on the words *claim* and *warrant*. The only two points to keep in mind if you try to vary them is that "the magic" of using this Talking Routine comes from (1) the two-part answer and (2) the words *not* being a part of regular daily student language, making students' arguments less personal.

FIRST ARGUMENTS—SOAPBOX DEBATES

To establish Talking Routines, we can introduce the first (and simplest) debate activity in the classroom—Soapbox Debates. If you walked into my classroom midyear, chances are high that you would see me start class with a version of this Soapbox Debate. Each student stands and says a sentence, using our Talking Routine, and then sits down. Those who are listening turn their eyes and knees toward each speaker, listening carefully and awaiting a chance to add to the debate.

Although the phrase "standing on your soapbox" may be unfamiliar to students these days, I tell my students that the title means standing up and stating your argument. It is as simple as that. (Some years I have given a one-minute history lesson as to the background of the phrase and an explanation of what a soapbox is if students were curious, but it is not something that is necessary.)

Here's how the routine works:

1. The teacher provides a debatable prompt.

   Examples could include anything nonmathematical ("The best movie is . . ." or "Dogs are the best pets") to something more content driven, such as "The best way to find slope is by . . ." or "The sequence 3, 6, . . . is an arithmetic sequence."

2. A student stands and states her thoughts using the "My claim is . . . , and my warrant is . . ." Talking Routine. Then that student sits down.

   For example, a student may stand and say, "My claim is that dogs are the best pets, and my warrant is that they are the most easily trained and loyal pets." Then she sits down. Or a student could stand and say, "The best way to find slope is to count the rise and run on a graph, and my warrant is counting on a picture is easy."

3. The next student stands and gives a claim and warrant, then sits down.

   The next student may stand and say, "My claim is also that dogs are the best pets, and my warrant is that they can cheer you up when you are sad." Or, the next student may disagree and say, "My claim is that dogs are not the best pets, and my warrant is that cats are more self-reliant and easier to care for."

4. Repeat step 3 with as many students as time permits or the debate allows.

INTRODUCING DEBATE

> **ARGUMENT—A STATEMENT MADE WITH SOUND REASONING. EVERY ARGUMENT HAS TWO KEY PARTS:**
>
> Claim—the controversial statement being made
> Warrant—the justification for the claim
>
> **ARGUMENT = CLAIM + WARRANT**
>
> "My CLAIM is _____,
> and my WARRANT is _____."

On the very first day, I post this slide to explain the definition of an argument and introduce the Talking Routine of claim and warrant. I start with a nonmathematical topic to ensure *all* students can engage. For instance, I like to start with questions like, "The best movie is . . ." or "The best musician is . . ." These are topics that all students usually have an answer for, allowing them to focus more on the routine than the one answer while easing math anxiety. (A friend of mine in New York loves comic books and has his middle school students first debate by asking which superhero has the best powers.) After the routine is established, we can transition to more mathematical questions/topics. As an example, the day I introduce Soapbox Debates, my first slide might look like this:

I go through one bullet point at a time, spending about two minutes on each one, having about four or five students share an argument for each bullet point before moving on to the next one.

LISTENING ROUTINES

The first day that I introduce debate, I focus solely on the Talking Routine of claim and warrant. However, the next time we do a debate, we also need to emphasize the importance of listening.

There are two major reasons we need to listen in a debate, in addition to being respectful to our classmates. The first reason is to avoid repetition. Because we have limited time in a debate, we must listen to what is being said so that we are not repeating an argument that has already been made. It is not only tedious to hear the same reasoning over and over again but also takes up precious class time. It's perfectly acceptable to have the same claim as someone who previously spoke, but each new argument has to have a new, unique warrant. For example, suppose a student begins the discussion about Figure 2.2 with:

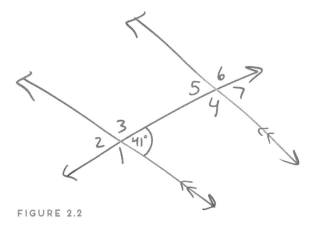

FIGURE 2.2

Edward: *I claim that Angle 5 is 41 degrees, and my warrant is that Angle 5 and the 41 are alternate interior angles.*

Another student could also talk about Angle 5, as long as the warrant has changed, such as:

Patricia: *I also claim that Angle 5 is 41 degrees, and my warrant is that Angles 5 and 2 are corresponding angles and Angle 2 is across from the 41.*

The second reason for listening carefully is so we can respond to the previous arguments. As we progress with debating in the classroom, there will be times where we can instruct students to give a claim and warrant specifically responding to the previous student's argument. Being able to summarize or quote something that was just said shows that the student was listening, and it makes the counterargument stronger.

Therefore, it is important that students have both Talking Routines and Listening Routines. My Listening Routines are straightforward: those who are not currently speaking during a debate turn their eyes and knees toward the speaker and actively listen. I focus on the "eyes and knees" part with students because it is the aspect I can see. When students say they are listening, they are quiet. We can't necessarily *see* that they are listening. However, they can show us and the speaker that they are attempting to listen by shifting their bodies. When students turn their eyes and knees toward the speaker, they are physically showing respect to the speaker and showing us that they know how to listen. That is all that I ask for because listening often follows naturally from turning to face the speaker. To paraphrase the great actor Constantin Stanislavski, physical action leads to the emotion. "You cannot follow the . . . external action sincerely and directly and not have the corresponding emotions" (Stanislavski 1936, 329). In other words, physically doing something, like stomping over toward another actor on stage, leads to the emotion or reaction desired (anger builds naturally from the stomping). In the classroom, having students perform a physical movement for listening often leads to active listening inherently. In doing the action, the desired listening follows.

While students are debating, we, as the teacher, should sit down and stay seated. We can call on students to facilitate the debate, but we do not want to draw focus. We want the student speaker to stand and be clearly visible, and we want the rest of the students to turn toward that speaker and listen actively.

It is easy for students to look toward the teacher if you are standing, and we want students to be speaking to one another, not to us. We want speakers to address their claims and warrants to the whole class. When we sit, we are a little harder to see, and students tend to more naturally address the class and look at other students. Additionally, we help model the Listening Routine of "eyes and knees" by sitting down and focusing our attention on the speakers.

We all have different spaces and different constraints that affect how we set up our classrooms. The physical set up of desks in a classroom can sometimes be a barrier to students turning to face the speaker. My room is currently set up with desks in a sort of horseshoe shape because I want students to be able to face one another easily. However, I have seen the "eyes and knees" routine work in many different classroom settings, my former classroom included. I used to have desks in pods of four, which allowed group-work activities to happen with ease. I eventually found that angling some of the groups at a slant allowed for easier listening movement in our class discussions and debates.

It can take some trial and error to figure out the ideal setup that makes both debate routines and group or pair work (or whatever other classroom routines you have) possible in a way that is not overly complicated. We want transitions into debates and discussions to be smooth.

I want to end this section by reiterating the importance of posting the Talking Routine "My claim is . . . , and my warrant is . . ." on all the walls of the classroom. This visibility is not only for the speaker but also for the listeners. The speaker can use the posted Talking Routine as a reminder of exactly how to begin. This reminder provides safety and empowerment, giving students some of the words to say. Additionally, the postings are also for the listeners who may be thoughtfully preparing an argument to go next. As everyone is shifting in their seats so that their eyes and knees are facing the speaker, there should be at least one posting of claim and warrant in their eyesight, which helps students stay focused on what they need to say.

A FEW POINTERS

A key component of debating is making the speaker stand. Although some students can be resistant at first, with a little friendly cajoling, most students oblige. After all, we are only asking them to stand and say one sentence before they can sit back down again, and we gave them the words to say for half the sentence. They just have to fill in the blanks after "My claim is" and "my warrant is." The first time a student stands can be scary, but once she stands up and speaks in class, she is more likely to do it again the next time we debate. That initial breaking-the-ice moment brings students more fully into the classroom debate culture. Quite quickly, fears of speaking to the class recede, and every student feels empowered to speak and debate in class.

Students standing and using the formal words of *claim* and *warrant* help to elevate the tone in the room and keep the discussion from becoming too casual. Also, if a student stands, it is easier for other students to see the speaker and show respect by turning eyes and knees toward the speaker. That said, based on the physical constraints of your classroom and your knowledge of your students, you will have to make a decision about what the speaker should do when stating an argument.

To help students feel safe and prepared to give an argument, I employ a few different strategies. First, I always allow a good amount of wait time. When I want to start class with a short Soapbox Debate, I have the questions we are going to debate on the board before we start class. As students enter class, they are asked to think about the statements silently and prepare an argument for each one. If they would like, they are welcome to write their answers down in their notebook. This preparation time allows students the opportunity to fully formulate what they are going to say and helps them remember what they wanted to say when they are called on.

Second, I begin by asking for volunteers to start the debate. There are almost always one or two students eager to share an opinion, and if I am concerned that my class may generally be on the quiet side, I may circulate around the room and prepare a few students to start the debate. Reading over their shoulders, I can see the arguments they have prepared, and I can quietly ask them if they would share when we begin the debate. This way I know that I have a few voices to get us started.

Additionally, I am open to cold-calling students. Like teachers who have popsicle sticks with student names, I have an index card for each student, and all of these cards together make a stack I call my "Cards of Math Destiny" (a name I took from math teachers who share online). I like to take a mix of volunteers and random names generated by my index cards when we debate. Although teachers debate whether they agree with the practice of cold-calling, I claim that it can be useful for introducing fresh voices and increasing student engagement. One of my personal rules about cold-calling is that it must be random. I do not want students to think I am picking on them. Rather, their destiny has been chosen by the cards!

There can always be a student who is terrified of public speaking, perhaps even more so in a math class, where fears and anxiety can strike hard. In the first week of school, I may let that student be an active listener, and I will have a one-on-one chat with that student to encourage him to participate. I call these one-on-one talks after class my "doorway chats." During a doorway chat with a reluctant speaker, I'll give the student the opportunity to prepare and rehearse ahead of time. For example, I'll pick an upcoming day for the student to participate ("I'd like you to give a claim and a warrant on Friday."), and give that student the question ahead of time ("Friday, I will ask what method you prefer to solve a system of equations. Do you think you could be ready for that? You could even write your sentence down in your notebook."). Often, the opportunity to prepare ahead of time removes the student's worries about speaking "on the spot," and he can successfully enter his first math debate.

A few last (hopefully) helpful notes on doing a Soapbox Debate:

- Keep it brief. Keep it simple. Students' (and teachers') initial concern is that this is going to be a large and complicated routine. Keeping the debates short and sweet helps students warm up to them. I like to have three to five students answer each question, and as the facilitator, I try to keep it moving, calling on the next volunteer or cold-calling the next student as soon as the current speaker finishes. I try to avoid too much lag time once we begin speaking, and I emphasize to the students that it is just one sentence—a claim and a warrant.

- Remind students that it is OK to repeat a claim, but their goal is to have a different warrant. Yes, you and I may have the same favorite movie (how cool is that!), but our reasons for loving that movie could be slightly or vastly different. Reminding students of this expectation alleviates the fears that they have to come up with a completely different answer. They don't. They just have to have a different reason for their claim.

- You control the timing. As you are facilitating the debate, you may notice that a certain question really doesn't allow for too many unique perspectives. So, you may end debate on one question (and perhaps go onto a second question) after only two or three students have spoken. This decision involves the teacher reading the room and the quality of the arguments. (We'll focus more on writing good questions for fuller debates in the coming chapters.)

RESOURCE: WHICH ONE DOESN'T BELONG?

Looking for a quick Soapbox Debate question to start your class? One of my favorite resources is the website "Which One Doesn't Belong?" (wodb.ca), which is a website curated by Canadian math teacher Mary Bourassa, inspired by Christopher Danielson's book, *Which One Doesn't Belong?* (2016). The examples there have four boxes, each filled with a similar number or picture or equation, like the one in Figure 2.3.

A	B
$y = 4x + 3$	$y = -4x + 5$
C	D
$y = \frac{1}{4}x + 5$	$y = 4x - 5$

FIGURE 2.3   MISHAAL SURTI

I label the boxes *A*, *B*, *C*, and *D*. Then, students give a claim and warrant why one of the four boxes does not belong. For instance, a student may say:

> Janice: *Box A doesn't belong because it is the only one with 3 as a y-intercept.*

The genius of Which One Doesn't Belong? (WODB) diagrams is that there is at least one warrant for each of the four boxes. In other words, there is a reason you could argue why each one could be the one that does not belong. Over time, my students grow to love WODB and try to come up with reasons for all four of the boxes, wanting to be the only speaker with a reason for one of the boxes.

As an example of a Soapbox Debate in my class, just the other day, I created the WODB example in Figure 2.4 as a warm-up in a trigonometry unit.

I labeled the boxes *A*, *B*, *C*, and *D*, starting in the top left corner with *A* and going across in each row, so the bottom right box was the last one, *D*. Student responses were:

> Barb: *My claim is Box A does not belong, and my warrant is that it is the only one that does not require trig stuff. You can just use Pythagorean theorem.*

> Teresa: *My claim is that Box B does not belong, and my warrant is that it is the only one that is a special right triangle. It's the only one you can do without a calculator.*

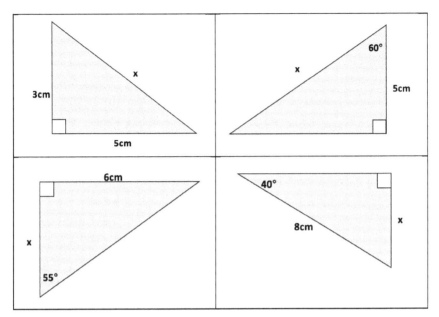

FIGURE 2.4

Pedro: *My claim is Box C does not belong, and my warrant is that it is the only one that does not involve the hypotenuse. So, you would use tangent.*

You can see from the responses of these students that they are homing in on key differences in the process for solving each of these triangles and using the math vocabulary I want them to use. The more students can talk about these problems, the deeper they will understand the processes for solving similar problems.

BONUS: WOW THE PARENTS!

I want to end this chapter with a thought about explaining debate to parents. In my experience, some parents are confused as to why their son or daughter is debating in math class, and they come to me with questions about why I do it. They often come from experiences where math only ever had a right or wrong answer, where the math teacher stood at the front of the room and did most of the talking, and they were not pressed to verbally practice explaining or reasoning. That said, parents are interested and genuinely curious how one could debate in math class.

One of my favorite activities is teaching parents to debate with the claim and warrant routine when they are in my classroom for a parent night. My current school calls it Back to School Night, where parents visit each of their child's teachers, following the schedule of their child for ten- to fifteen-minute segments. When I get a group of parents in my room, I quickly teach them the Talking Routine of "My claim is . . . , and my warrant is . . . ," and then I have them debate. I like to do a WODB as a warm-up, and sometimes I further debate with the parents, using questions about helping their child. I use prompts such as "The best way I can help my daughter excel at math is . . ." or "The most important skill my child needs to learn in this class is . . ."

In working with parents, they (like their children) quickly grow to understand and appreciate the debate structures. The debate structure often opens up a jovial conversation about encouraging reasoning, justification, problem solving, and estimation at home. The parents are grateful for the advice that they get from one another, and they enjoy the debating atmosphere too!

QUESTION ROUND

A n elementary teacher friend recently challenged me to make the closed question

2 + 2 =

into a debatable one. Assuming the objective was to assess student understanding of addition, I replied with a few options for the new question:

- What is the best way to model this?
- What is the silliest mistake we can make when solving this problem?
- Who can come up with the coolest story for this problem?
- What is the most interesting way I could add numbers to this problem and still get the same solution?

And the list goes on. By opening up the question to opinions and interpretations, students are not only developing arguments but also increasing their engagement with the problem.

So, how do you start doing this? We have been exploring what debatable moments look and sound like: students engaging with mathematics and each other through clear and brief verbal routines, allowing us teachers to listen closely and minimize our talk time. Now it is time for us to turn our attention to what the teacher needs to do in his or her preparation to make these debatable moments happen. What kinds of questions will engage students in rich mathematical debates? As written, most questions in math textbooks do not spark lively discussion among our students. So how might we transform, adapt, or create new questions that will engage students in debate about content?

CONTENT OBJECTIVES

First off, I want to emphasize that when a class debates, student learning of math content is at the forefront of the activity. We do not want students to debate just for the sake of saying that our students talk in class. So, we need to write questions with a clear, mathematical objective in mind. For example, suppose you were working with students on domain and range of functions. You would not ask students, *Who drew the messiest graph?* because that may have nothing to do with

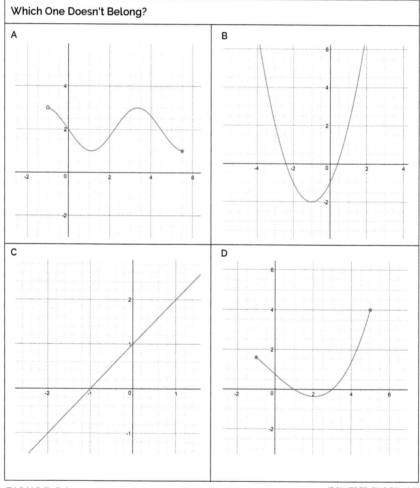

FIGURE 3.1   (POWERED BY DESMOS)

[30]

the objective for the lesson. Depending on your goal, you might consider these options instead:

- If your goal is to strengthen student vocabulary around graphs and functions, then you could have students debate a Which One Doesn't Belong? like the one I created in Figure 3.1. It would encourage your students to use words such as *closed*, *open*, *maximum*, and *infinity* (among other great mathy words).

- However, if your goal was to clarify misconceptions about closed and open intervals, you might show examples of incorrect student work and ask, *Who has the best mistake?* as in Figures 3.2A and 3.2B.

Draw a graph with the domain (−5,5) and a range (−3,3).

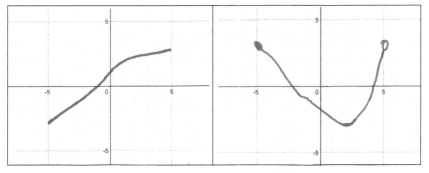

FIGURE 3.2A   FIGURE 3.2B

The objective guides the question. We want the math *learning* to be the point of debating in class. Having clear objectives for each lesson and activity helps keep you laser focused when selecting or writing a debatable moment. Once you have your objective in mind, you can create a debatable question.

WHAT MAKES A QUESTION DEBATABLE?

Many of us struggle to have students discuss math problems because textbook questions traditionally only have one answer. For example:

What is the slope of the line $y = 2x − 8$?

This is a closed question, and it will not engender a debate (let alone much discussion). Closed questions have their place in math class—I am not arguing

to get rid of closed-ended questions. Rather, some of the time, we need debatable questions to get students arguing and critiquing the reasoning of others.

To create debatable moments in class, we need to open questions to students' opinions and give students a chance to have something to say. We need open-ended questions—those with more than one answer—and "opinion-ended" questions—ones that allow for students to develop arguments. Think back to our definition of *claim* in Chapter 2: a controversial statement that has the potential for opposing sides. To realize that potential, we need to ask questions that generate multiple answers or opinions.

Suppose, for example, our objective is to help students understand the importance of slope. Going back to the question about the line $y = 2x - 8$, we could ask questions like: *What is the most important number in the equation of a line?* or *What is the worst mistake you can make when graphing this line?* Take a moment to think of a few examples of arguments that your students might come up with.

What made these questions debatable are the word choices. First, notice how both of the examples allow for multiple "correct" answers. For example, for the first question, students could respond:

> Li: *I claim that the number 2 is the most important number, and my warrant is that it is the slope. It tells you how much the line slants.*

or

> Manny: *I claim that the −8 is the most important number. My warrant is −8 is the y-intercept and that tells you where to start graphing.*

The wording of the question has an ambiguity to it that allows students to take a variety of stances. Additionally, the phrasing has a personal draw that heightens engagement and almost forces opinions to be formed. How can we ask *What is most important?* and *not* have human beings form opinions in their minds?

If students share multiple, solid arguments, your objective is met. Students (and not the teacher) have explained the importance of slope. Even more exciting, the debate usually surpasses your objective because the class has discussed a lot more than just the slope. Students may also have recalled vocabulary like y-intercept and possibly discussed ideas for graphing, such as scaling the axes.

BEST/WORST STARTER

One of the quickest ways to make a question debatable is to start your statement with "The best . . ." or "The worst . . ." For instance, suppose you're having students practice solving linear equations with distribution such as:

$$\frac{1}{3}(x-8) = 2$$

If you want students to discuss and debate this problem (either before or after solving it), you could create a debatable moment by giving students one of the following statements and asking them to fill in the blank.

The best first step is _____.

The worst first step is _____.

Some students may prefer to distribute first. Others may talk about dividing by one-third (or multiplying by 3) on both sides. Both are valid first steps, but adding a word like *best* allows students to have an opinion about their method.

> **Dereka:** *My claim is that multiplying by 3 on both sides is the best first step, and my warrant is because I hate fractions—I want to get rid of the fraction as soon as possible. Then it is easier for me to do the rest of the math quickly.*

As another example, consider my precalculus class. We began by exploring the parameters of sine and cosine graphs for two or three days. I wanted to start the next class with a quick and informal check for understanding, to see how well students were progressing. Initially, I planned to ask students to complete the following:

GRAPH THE FUNCTION

$$y = 8\sin\left(\frac{\pi}{15}x\right) + 10$$

CHAPTER 3: QUESTION ROUND

It was a straightforward problem, meant to assess students' understandings of how each of the numbers in the equation affects the shape of a sine graph. I wanted students to be able to explain the amplitude, period, and vertical shift and how they would scale the axes. However, there is not much room for opinion in this problem, so I employed the Best/Worst Starter idea to change it to a question this way:

THE BEST WAY TO START GRAPHING A SINE FUNCTION IS . . .

$$y = 8\sin\left(\frac{\pi}{15}x\right) + 10$$

My students' responses to this warm-up were more interesting and revealing than if students had just graphed the function.

> **Bryana:** *My claim is the best way to graph a sine function is to first look at the amplitude, and my warrant is because it gets you the height.*

> **Xialin:** *My claim is the pi 15 thing is the best way to graph a sine function. My warrant is that it's what you use to make the x-axis work.*

> **Julion:** *I claim the plus 10 is the best way to start graphing because that is the starting point. The midline? From there you can just graph a sine graph and use the amplitude.*

> **Mr. Luzniak:** *I love these arguments! Can I pause for a moment and ask someone to clarify one of the recent arguments with our math vocabulary?*

> **Jennah:** *I claim like Julion that the vertical shift is the best thing to graph a sine function, and my warrant is that it tells you how far up to start on the y. Then if you add and subtract 8, the amplitude, you will know how high to go. And low.*

Notice how students were struggling with both the vocabulary they need and with ordering the steps for starting to graph. As the teacher in the room, I interrupted the debate to push for more precise math vocabulary, but I did not comment on the ordering of steps. Once we had elicited some student ideas in the debate, I asked the class to try to graph the sine function in parentheses. Giving students a few minutes for quick debate not only increased student engagement and argumentation in the class but also helped many students review the main ideas and clear up some misconceptions. Students who were unsure where to start got support from classmates on how to approach graphing sine functions, which increased their access to the mathematics. I was able to listen in on student thinking and get a sense of where my class was. It was a win-win moment for us all.

MORE DEBATE-Y WORDS

Adding a brief Best/Worst statement makes a straightforward question debatable because the students can now have opinions about what is *best* (or *worst*) for the given situation. *Best* and *worst* are not the only words that can invoke opinion, but they are my go-to starters. Following is a fuller list of words that can turn a closed mathematical question or statement into a debatable one.

• Best/Worst	• Weirdest/Coolest
• Should/Could	• Hardest/Easiest
• Biggest/Smallest	• Most/Least

These words are superlatives and assertions that push students to form opinions, and these opinions, in turn, create debatable moments in class. Here are some examples of questions teachers have written using these starters:

- What do you think is the *most* common mistake when solving this problem?
- What is the *weirdest* mistake someone could have made on the test?
- What *should* be the last step when graphing a line?
- Which shape do you think will have the *most* area? The *least* perimeter?
- What is the *coolest* parent graph?
- What was the *hardest* topic in this unit?
- What is the *biggest* mistake students could make when adding fractions?

- What is the *easiest* way to estimate the area under this curve?

This list can help you write a debate-worthy question for your next lesson. Keeping your mathematical objective in mind, try choosing a superlative to create a question where students can form opinions. Then, after you try it out in class, reflect on what you learned from your students' responses.

MAKE IT DEBATABLE!

We can write our own original, debatable questions with the previous list. We can also quickly transform a closed question from a textbook, resource, or already developed lesson plan into one that leads to a debate. Some examples of this transformation:

$\dfrac{1}{2} + \dfrac{3}{4} =$	What is the *coolest* way to visualize this problem?
Solve for x: $2x + 3 = 3x - 4.$	What is the *most* common mistake you might see in this problem?
Find the radius of a circle with an area of 24π square units.	What is the *hardest* part about this question?
Solve for $x: 0 = x^2 + 3x$	What is the *best* method to solve this equation?
Determine $\sin\left(-\frac{9\pi}{4}\right)$	What *should* be the first step in solving this problem?
Find $f'(4)$ when $f(x) = 3\sqrt{x} + 1$	What is the *biggest* mistake you could make in solving this problem?

With practice, it can become easier, almost second nature, to use our list of superlatives to reword closed questions into debatable ones. Daily! I certainly use them over and over in my lessons.

As useful as these words are, there are other ways we can create debatable questions and moments in the classroom. Let's explore some techniques together.

ALWAYS, SOMETIMES, NEVER

Some of the curricula you use or the resources you rely on already have "thinking" or "discussion" questions written for you. These can often be great questions to use once you have a Talking Routine (like claim and warrant) fixed in your class. I encourage you to use quality premade questions when you can.

One way to ensure you will generate debate about the "discussion" question is to ask students if the statement is always true, sometimes true, or never true. For example, are the following statements always, sometimes, or never true?

- When you add or subtract 10, the ones digit does not change.
- The fraction with the larger numerator is the larger fraction.
- Every shape has a line of symmetry.
- The variable must always be on the left side of the equal sign.
- If Jan gets a 30% raise and Matt gets a 25% raise, Jan got the bigger raise.
- A triangle can have two obtuse angles.
- 4π and $2x\pi$ are co-terminal angles on the unit circle.
- Lisa's velocity is given by the function $y = 4x$. Zane's velocity is given by the function $y = 6x$. Therefore, after 5 seconds, Zane will be the farthest away.

These questions often evoke great conversations as students claim that the statement is either always, sometimes, or never true and then try to justify their claims with warrants. For example, you might hear in a geometry class:

> **Lorn:** *My claim is that "A triangle can have two obtuse angles" is never true, and my warrant is that that would mean two angles are more than 90 degrees. There is no way that can happen if the angles have to add up to 180.*

And in a precalculus class, you could hear:

> **Melani:** *I claim 4 pi and 2x pi are always co-terminal angles, and my warrant is that when you plug in numbers for x you get 2 pi, 4 pi, 6 pi, and so on. These are all co-terminal.*

> **Kyra:** *My claim is that 4 pi and 2x pi are sometimes co-terminal angles because when you plug in a fraction like $\frac{1}{2}$ for x, it is in a different place in the unit circle.*

What constitutes an acceptable warrant really depends on the experiences of your students and your goals in that moment. Whether or not students have seen formal proofs before, they intuitively know what it means to be convincing. As their teacher, with knowledge of your students, you can push students to increase the rigor. You can set the bar for solid reasoning. Is a counterexample a reasonable expectation? Is a formal proof what you are building toward? With all debates, what students say may be quite rigorous, or you can challenge students to heighten their arguments with more mathematically solid warrants.

USING STUDENT MISTAKES

One of my favorite ways to get students talking and debating in class is to share student mistakes. You can take mistakes from two different students and debate about the *best mistake* or *coolest mistake*. These questions are usually sources of rich discussion and learning for students. Not only that, but they also help create a classroom culture where mistake making is acceptable and a valuable part of the learning process.

For example, if you were to ask students to convert an angle of 5 radians into degree measurement, that would be a closed question. If you wanted to spark a debate, you might include examples of student mistakes, as in Figures 3.3A–3.3C and ask, *Who has the best mistake?*

$$5\pi\left(\frac{180}{\pi}\right) = 900°$$

FIGURE 3.3A

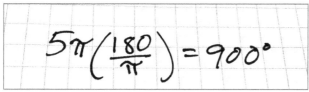

$$5° \times \frac{\pi}{180} = \frac{5\pi}{180} = 0.09$$

FIGURE 3.3B

$$5rad \approx \frac{5\pi}{3}$$

$$\frac{5\pi}{3} \cdot \frac{180}{\pi} = \frac{300}{1} = 300°$$

FIGURE 3.3C

As another example, in my calculus class recently, we were wrapping up a unit on limits. On the day of the quiz, I created a warm-up for the class to debate (see following slide) that consisted of common mistakes students had made on recent homework problems. This debate lasted just over ten minutes, and it was a great review for students who were still struggling with misconceptions. To engage in the debate, students had to first work out the correct answers. (There were a few students who were convinced that one of the problems was actually correct and that I was tricking them.) Then, they had to figure out what could have led to the mistake pictured. Last, they had to develop an argument for which one was the best mistake. This process highlighted a lot of misconceptions, and students were discussing these common errors with one another, clarifying understanding together.

LET'S DEBATE! WHICH ONE HAS THE BEST MISTAKE?

a) $\lim\limits_{x \to 2} \dfrac{x^2 - x}{x + 3} = \infty$

c) $\lim\limits_{x \to 2} \dfrac{x^2 - 2x}{x - 2} = DNE$

b) $\lim\limits_{x \to \infty} \dfrac{4x^2 + x}{9x - x^2} = \infty$

d) $\lim\limits_{x \to 0} \dfrac{\sin(x)}{x} = DNE$

Note: DNE means "does not exist."

USING STUDENTS' OWN WORDS

I try to have debatable moments, even very brief ones, daily in my class. They can take the form of a short warm-up question or a writing question on a worksheet or quiz. Anytime students have to convince someone—whether that is a classmate, the teacher, or a generic third person—is a debatable moment.

An added bonus of having students regularly debate ideas in math class is that unplanned debatable moments can also come up. Sometimes a student may say something we were not expecting that causes me or the class to pause, think, and begin a spontaneous debate. For instance, I once had a middle school student say:

I notice that when you tear a piece off of a shape, you reduce its area and perimeter.

Is this true? Where did this idea come from? This was a great moment for students to turn and talk for a minute or two. Then, we started a brief Soapbox Debate, where students shared their ideas:

Daquan: *I claim that this is true, and my warrant is that if you take a square and cut off a piece, you get a smaller area.*

Kati: *I claim that this is sometimes true. My warrant is because if you zigzag when you tear off a piece, you get more perimeter.*

This was a brief debate in my class that I cut short and asked students to ponder at home. However, I also could have allowed more time in the moment for students to discuss and explore the statement. Depending on the time you have available and the importance of the topic, you might adjust your lesson to allow this time. Perhaps your students have more misconceptions than you realized, and they need to debate a bit longer, as they work through the confusion. Or, as happened in my case, both the teacher and the students needed time to process the misunderstandings. I tabled the debate until the next class, giving myself an opportunity to follow up with a planned discussion the following day. I used the delay to give myself time to check in with colleagues, gathering information from those who had taught my current students, and collaborating on ways to proceed with my next lesson. It was clear there were many different directions the conversation could take.

When debating the statement, my students got into a discussion of the word *and*, wondering whether they had to explain both perimeter and area simultaneously or if it was two different questions. When I have shared this statement with adults at conferences, we have discussed whether *shape* implies two-dimensional objects only, or if we can explore what happens with three-dimensional objects (or even four-dimensional ones!). We have even gotten into semantic discussions about the word *tear*. What does that mean exactly? Can you tear in three or four dimensions? Is there a precise mathematical term we can use? Look at all that we've had to say about one student's statement. Imagine how validated that student, and hopefully the class, felt after seeing how I value students' conjectures by spending time on them.

ARE CLOSED QUESTIONS EVER DEBATABLE?

Debatable questions have multiple answers and opinions, like *Which one doesn't belong?* or *What is the best method for finding the area of this irregular shape?* These questions have multiple valid answers or approaches, and students can form differing opinions about them.

On the other hand, closed questions have a single answer. Closed questions are not exactly debatable. However, throughout this book, you can see that some of my examples are actually closed questions. I want to clarify that I include them in my list of debate-worthy examples anyway because I know from experience that they can spark good discussion in the classroom. Many students may initially have differing ideas of the solution, and their misconceptions are what cause a debate. For example, consider asking students to discuss the truth of the following statement:

Squaring a number makes the number bigger.

Some students may wonder if they can find a counterexample. However, most students—or even the entire class—may initially feel that the statement is true. Thus, even though the statement has a definite truth value (of false), the class can explore, discuss, and debate. Having an established culture for debate in the classroom makes discussion of these common misconceptions work well.

Other examples of debate-worthy misconceptions include:

- Can two numbers add up to nothing?
- True or false: Adding fractions always gives you another fraction.
- Can the height of a triangle be a slanted line?
- True or false: Square roots always make a number smaller.
- Is there a difference between $-x^2$ and $\left(-x\right)^2$?
- Are these all equivalent: $\sin^2 x$, $\sin x^2$, $\left(\sin x\right)^2$?
- True or false: $_nC_r = {_nC_{n-r}}$

In each of these examples, although the question I am asking the class has only one answer, my understanding of my students' knowledge and misconceptions tells me the question could lead to (usually, but not always!) a quality debatable moment. Having debate routines in place allows these unplanned moments to easily turn into a debate or a discussion. Some poking or prodding with questions like *What if we use negative numbers? What about fractions? Can we try to draw strange examples?* can get students questioning their initial solutions, and eventually we get a second opinion on the possible answer.

As another example, consider Figure 3.4. If you were to ask students to find the area of the triangle, that would be a closed question. Combining this closed question with student "mistakes" in Figure 3.5 leads to a debatable moment with: *Who has the best mistake?*

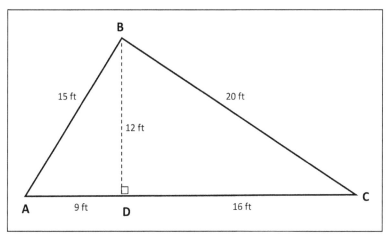

FIGURE 3.4

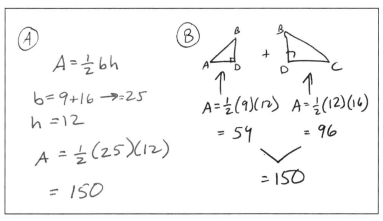

FIGURE 3.5

Notice that there actually are no mistakes here. However, knowledge of student misconceptions at this point lead me to believe this question would engender a debate. For example, we might hear students respond (mathematically incorrectly) to the question of the best mistake with:

> Netta: *I claim the first one has the best, and my warrant is because they used the wrong sides. You're supposed to use 15 and 20.*

or

> Roberta: *I claim the second one is the best mistake, and my warrant is that you can't change the problem to two triangles.*

These statements allow us as a class to discuss some misconceptions in finding the area of a triangle. The question is not technically debatable, but knowledge of students' confusions led to it becoming a debate activity.

So, please, forgive me if I continue to mix some closed questions in with truly debatable questions in my examples. In my class, I may allow a second opinion on a problem that only has one answer.

SO MANY QUESTIONS

In this chapter, we have talked about making questions debatable by using Best/Worst Starters; introducing "debate-y" words; framing questions as Always, Sometimes, Never; using students' mistakes or their own words; and debating misconceptions. Armed with these tools, let's take a question on multiplying integers, such as $3(-4) = $ ___, and make it debatable.

Solve $3(-4) = $ ___

- What is the best first step to solve this problem?
- What is the coolest way to model this problem?
- What is the easiest mistake you can make in solving this problem?
- Will there always, sometimes, or never be negative solutions?
- Which student had the best mistake? (See Figures 3.6A and 3.6B.)
- A student said, "When there's more than one negative, the answer is positive." Is that true?
- Does multiplication always result in a larger number?

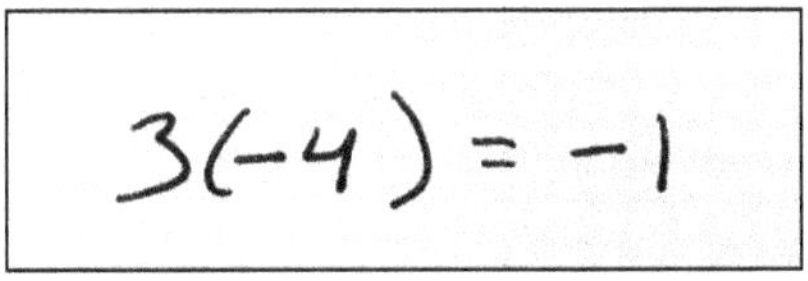

FIGURE 3.6A

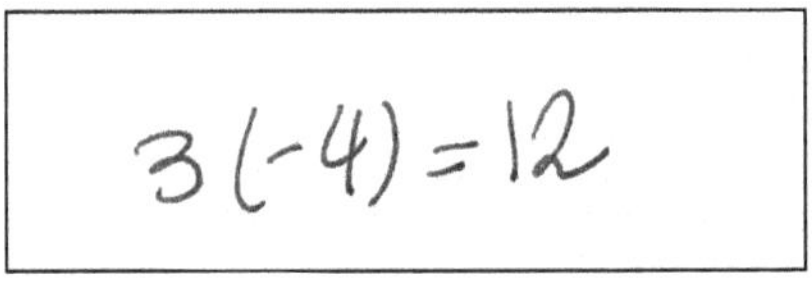

FIGURE 3.6B

Similarly, we could also consider a question on the quadratic formula, such as solving for x in the equation: $x^2 + x = 12$.

Solve for x: $x^2 + x = 12$.

- What is the best first step in solving this problem?
- What is the easiest method for solving this equation?
- What is most common mistake someone can make when solving this problem?
- Will there always, sometimes, or never be two solutions?
- Which student had the best mistake? (See Figures 3.7A and 3.7B.)
- Let's debate: "Some equations have two real number answers. Some have two imaginary answers. It isn't possible to have one real and one imaginary answer."
- True or false: $x^2 + x - 12 = 0$, $0 = 12 - x^2 - x$, and $0 = 12 + x^2 - x$ are all the same.

Notice the variety of open and closed questions that could spark a discussion and debate in your math classroom. Those are just seven examples of ways to make the question more debatable. Can you think of a few more options?

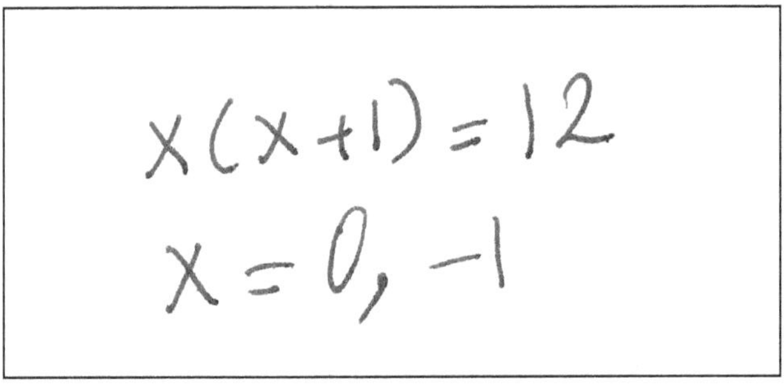

FIGURE 3.7A

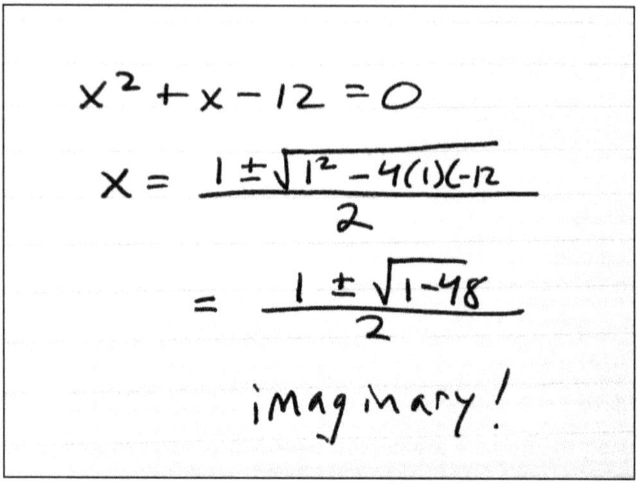

$$x^2 + x - 12 = 0$$

$$x = \frac{1 \pm \sqrt{1^2 - 4(1)(-12)}}{2}$$

$$= \frac{1 \pm \sqrt{1-48}}{2}$$

imaginary!

FIGURE 3.7B

DEBATE EVERYTHING!

Every time I work with teachers, I say that any math problem can become debatable. I make this broad claim partly to be controversial when talking about a subject that many (especially people outside our profession) believe to be unambiguous. I also say it because I want to push teachers to focus a little less on the correct answer and a little more on students' abilities to discuss and debate the concepts and processes.

I always challenge teachers to stump me—to come up with a math question for students that I *cannot* turn into a debatable moment. Although I would happily accept being stumped by an idea, I have yet to hear a question that I could not turn into a debatable moment. I say this not to brag, but to encourage you to think more openly about the questions you ask, about what you see as a closed question. Let your mind be open to making statements more debatable, and if you get stuck, send me a message or a tweet (@cluzniak, #DebateMath). Let's help one another raise the bar for debating math.

CHAPTER 4

CROSS-EXAMINATION

I f you are nervous about giving up class time for student discussion or giving students the freedom to share opinions—know you are not alone.

It was almost ten years ago when I decided to try having students debate a warm-up question in my class. The idea made me incredibly nervous—I was in a New York City public school with roughly thirty students in the room. What chaos would ensue if I let the students start debating?

Nevertheless, I believed that a debate would be good for my students. I believed that talking about math and developing arguments were valuable practices. So, I set my mind to try *one* brief debate moment. I spent two weeks planning for my first warm-up Soapbox Debate. I worked out the question I wanted to ask as a warm-up, and I rehearsed how I was going to explain the claim and warrant Talking Routine. In the days leading up to my planned debate, I went over the moment again and again in my mind, thinking of all the ways this could go wrong.

Then, I did it in class, and it was not a disaster. In fact, it went well, and my students ate it up! They were engaged and excited. Many hands went in the air the minute I said students had to share an opinion. I spent about five to seven minutes at the start of class allowing my students to have a voice and express themselves, and nothing went wrong.

The minute the debate was over, we went back into practicing whatever topic it was we were working on (I want to say it was graphing lines, but my memory is hazy now), and I breathed a sigh of relief. It was mid-October, and I had been working up to that moment since the start of the school year. Debate was the one new thing I wanted to try. I was glad it went well, but

the bridge thickness
how does the
change?
Breaking Weight
2 3 4 5
Bridge Thickness

then I took a break for a few weeks before building up the courage to try it again. To the students, debate may have been just another activity we did in class. They did not know how nervous I was or how much I prepared for each debate.

That first year, I only had students debate maybe three or four times during the warm-up part of class. It was exciting for the students, but too new for me to do too often. I say this to emphasize that my classroom full of debate did not happen overnight. I encourage all teachers to start small—once a week or once a month can be a comfortable amount of change when trying something new. Risk taking in the classroom definitely takes courage and perseverance, and not every debate will go smoothly. However, we will never know how it will go until we try, and even if the debate does not go smoothly, the experience gives us something to reflect on, so we can figure out what needs to happen to make it work. We all have to play with and tweak the ideas to work for us, in our situation, for our students.

I eased into classroom debates slowly, and with each attempt, my confidence and understanding grew. Each year, I added more debatable moments, slowly building larger activities and debates as summative assessments, and now, debate is a staple of my classroom. Ask any of my students, and they will tell you (perhaps with a loving eye roll) that "Mr. Luzniak loves to make us debate."

Hopefully, the first three chapters of this book have illuminated how to begin. With some brief but explicit student directions (Talking Routines) and some slight changes to our questions (Best/Worst Starters), we can create short debates about math throughout the school year. This may be a good point to pause your reading and start trying things out. Take your time. (I did!)

When you are hungry for more, this chapter will extend the ideas discussed in the previous chapters, providing more activities, variations, and structures to keep debates fresh, deepening the work we have begun.

CIRCLE DEBATES

Have you tried out some Soapbox Debates and are wondering, *What next?* Let's explore! Once I have devoted a few days to introducing students to the Soapbox Debate Routine, I start to add slight variations. I call the first variation a "Circle Debate," and the goal is to teach students to listen to one another and summarize what they have heard. Like in a Soapbox Debate, students will stand at their desks and deliver a claim and a warrant to the class, as they are called on. The only change is that after the first person has spoken, each successive person will first summarize the previous speaker's argument before giving their own claim and warrant. I offer to students, as an addition to our Talking Routine, the sentence starter "I heard . . ." Often in a Circle Debate, I will have the speaker call on the next student to participate.

Here's how the routine works:

1. The teacher states a debatable question. For example: *What is the best way to solve a quadratic equation (such as $0 = x^2 + 6x + 8$)?*

2. A student stands and states his thoughts as a sentence using the "My claim is . . . , and my warrant is . . ." Talking Routine. Then that student sits down.

   Hanita: *My claim is that factoring is the best way to solve a quadratic equation, and my warrant is that it is faster and easier.*

3. The next student stands, summarizes the previous student's argument, and then gives her own claim and warrant.

   Corey: *I heard Hanita say that she prefers factoring because it is quicker. However, I claim that the quadratic formula is the best, and my warrant is it always works. Also, I don't like trying to figure out factoring.*

4. The speaker calls on the next student to participate, sits down, and the new student repeats step 3. We continue this routine with as many students as time permits or the debate allows.

   Suh: *I heard that Corey likes the quadratic formula, but I don't. I claim that Hanita was right that factoring is faster, and my warrant is that once you factor you can just see your solutions. You don't have to do anymore work.*

   Ali: *Suh just said she likes factoring because it is easier, and she can see the answer. But I claim you should complete the square. My warrant is that completing the square makes it easy to see the picture of the graph too. So you can easily see if there are no solutions.*

Having students actively listen and summarize what they heard is not easy. So often, students are not actually listening to one another; they are just thinking about what they want to say next. Requiring students to summarize the previous speaker forces them to listen to what is being said. I also like to have students self-reflect on how they did the first time in a Circle Debate as a brief exit slip so they can think about their listening and summarizing skills.

POINT/COUNTERPOINT

As students become more comfortable with debate in math class, I emphasize to them that a good debater is ready to argue multiple sides of an issue. So, when I reach a point where students are ready, I introduce a second variation to the Soapbox Debate, one we call *Point/Counterpoint*, where students are forced to come up with arguments for opposing sides of the debate.

A Point/Counterpoint Debate can work a lot like a Soapbox Debate, with two key differences. First, the question asked can only have two sides to argue. Second, once a student has given a claim and a warrant, the next speaker must *always* provide a claim for the opposite side of the debate. This pattern continues, where each consequent speaker must argue the opposite of the previous speaker. Thus, a Point/Counterpoint Debate involves a continual back-and-forth of the two sides of the argument, and students must be ready to argue for whatever side is required when they are called on.

The first time I introduce this version of a debate, I tell students I am modeling it after a game my friends and I played as children: *Would You Rather?* In this game, you could be asked a question like: *Would you rather be caught in the rain without an umbrella or be forced to wear winter clothes on a hot day?* Then the Point/Counterpoint Routine could go like this:

1. The teacher states a debatable question. For example: *Would you rather be caught in the rain without an umbrella or be forced to wear winter clothes on a hot day?*

2. A student stands and states her thoughts as a sentence using the "My claim is . . . , and my warrant is . . ." Talking Routine. Then that student sits down.

Karyn: *My claim is that it is better to wear winter clothes on a hot day, and my claim is that being warm is better than being wet and cold. Plus, in the shade you'll be fine.*

3. The next student stands and gives his own claim and warrant for the *opposite* claim. No matter which side the student would personally advocate for, he must argue for the opposing side of the debate.

    Guyton: *I claim it is better to be caught in the rain. My warrant is it would be refreshing and romantic!*

4. The next student goes back to the first side of the argument.

    Elisa: *I claim that I would rather wear winter clothes on a hot day, and my warrant is that, once I get to school, I can take some layers off, and I won't be soaked like people in the rain.*

5. Students continue arguing, always taking the opposite claim of the previous speaker.

    Finn: *I claim that I would rather be caught in the rain, and my warrant is that sweating in the heat makes you all gross and sweaty. Getting wet from the rain is like cleaning up after a shower.*

Here is a more mathematical version of the Point/Counterpoint Routine:

Question: *Suppose you were trying to find 45% of 80. Would you rather determine this by setting up a proportion or by converting the percentage to a decimal and multiplying?*

Reggie: *I claim that I would rather set up a proportion. My warrant is that it is easy to set up 45 over 100 equals x over 80.*

Jill: *I claim that I would rather convert to a decimal, and my warrant is that it is quick to convert 45% to 0.45 and multiply with a calculator times 80. I think it's faster.*

Billi: *I claim that I would rather set up a proportion because I like to cross multiply.*

Depending on the question, this could continue back and forth for as long as time allows. Also, we can combine Point/Counterpoint with Circle Debates for extra levels of depth, having students summarize *and* be ready for either side of the argument.

RESOURCE: WOULD YOU RATHER MATH?

Once my students are comfortable with debating, they start to look forward to the challenge of Point/Counterpoint Debates. As their teacher, it is not always easy to come up with rich questions that have two specific sides. I like to use John Stevens's site "Would You Rather . . . ?" Math (wouldyourathermath.com) to find engaging questions.

On the website, you can find a wealth of questions that you can use in your classroom immediately. See Figures 4.1 and 4.2 for some examples that I have used. In each case, the question is, *Would you rather?* With Talking Routines already established in your class and a Would You Rather? math question, the class should quickly be able to jump into a debate.

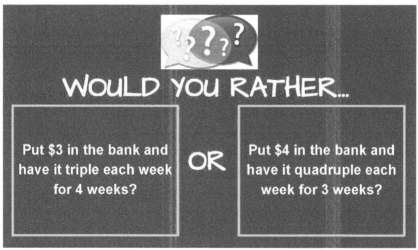

WOULD YOU RATHER...

Put $3 in the bank and have it triple each week for 4 weeks? OR Put $4 in the bank and have it quadruple each week for 3 weeks?

FIGURE 4.1   JOHN STEVENS, WOULDYOURATHERMATH.COM

Push a 20 kg box up the hypotenuse of triangle A or triangle B?

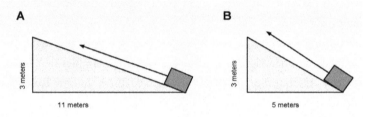

FIGURE 4.2   JOHN STEVENS, WOULDYOURATHERMATH.COM

DEBATE CARDS

Debate is not only for whole-class activities. There are times when we want students to work in pairs or groups, and any of the previously mentioned activities could be modified for partners or small groups. Just as we have students turn and talk with a partner, we can have students turn and *debate* with a partner. Additionally, we can use what I call a Debate Cards activity.

Debate Cards are for pairs (or maybe two pairs in a group of four), and they require some preparation from the teacher. For setup, I make a set of five to ten cards for each pair (the same problems for each group) with a similar type of problem. For instance, in a geometry unit on area of irregular shapes, I could use the cards in Figures 4.3–4.7.

During class, I pass out the stack of premade cards to each pair (facedown). I then ask each pair (or group) to choose someone to be Partner A. The other person will be Partner B. Then, I reveal the directions:

- Partner A needs to show how to find the area of the irregular shape (the blue area) using the adding method (breaking the irregular shape up into smaller pieces and adding up the area of each of the smaller chunks) and then provide a warrant as to why their method is the best.

FIGURE 4.3

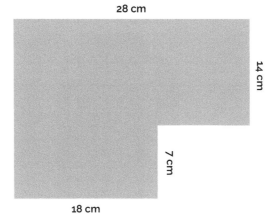

28 cm

14 cm

7 cm

18 cm

FIGURE 4.4

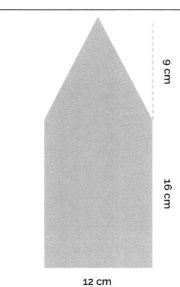

9 cm

16 cm

12 cm

FIGURE 4.5

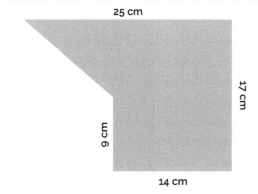

25 cm

17 cm

9 cm

14 cm

FIGURE 4.6

10 cm

14 cm

FIGURE 4.7

12 cm

12 cm

- Partner B needs to show how to find the same area using the subtraction method (finding the area of the larger shape and subtracting the area of the smaller "white space" shapes) and then provide a warrant as to why their method is the best.

The partners then flip over the top card, solve the given problem each in their own method, and use their work to argue why their method is best. Sometimes my students prefer to solve the problems separately and silently in their assigned method and then share work as they debate. Other times, students like to talk through their method of solving the problems one at a time and end it with their argument. I have no strong preference on which way students can proceed, and I often leave it up to them. Students then proceed to the next card in the deck, working through one problem at a time.

The great part about this version of the debate is that each student gets a lot of practice using a particular method and creating arguments for that method, and if I wanted to give students time practicing both methods, I could have partners switch roles midway through the deck. Also, with purposeful choices of problems, students can see how certain problems may be easier with one method over the other. Sometimes, to be particularly pointed in my goal, I like to add a card (like the one in Figure 4.7) that students can only solve using one method (in this case, the subtraction method) to purposely stump students who were assigned the other method (in this case, the addition method). Students then naturally feel and discuss the need to have multiple methods and not just rely on one method. To further emphasize the importance of flexibility, I may also add an example to the deck where the opposite is true: in this example, the card in Figure 4.6 is much more easily solved with the addition method and would stump the students who were assigned the subtraction method. That student who likes to latch onto one method and just repeat that method over and over will (hopefully) see the need for learning multiple methods.

These Debate Cards are an effective replacement for rote practice problems, and they can be used in many areas. On my website (luzniak.com), there is a growing number of examples of Debate Cards created by many teachers across the Math-Teacher-Blog-o-Sphere (#MTBoS). Feel free to explore, and even create (and share) your own!

Let me add a quick word about student accountability. When I share these Debate Cards, teachers often ask how to keep groups accountable. Some options are as follows:

- We can take notes on clipboards as we circulate around the room. Using a class list or seating chart, we can systematically notice how each student is doing. This is a nice formative assessment for us, although it is harder to do in larger classes. I like to have two or three days of debate activities, giving me several days to complete my goal of checking in with each and every student, holding myself accountable to know where every student is in his or her learning.

- Students could be required to hand in their work for each problem at the end of the activity. Before debating each card, students could solve their given problem and record all their work on a graphic organizer. Students could also be required to write their arguments at the end of their work.

- Each pair could have a master sheet where they keep track of the argument they found the strongest for each card. After working through and debating each card, the students can write down the "winning" argument, the one that they both agree was the best for a given card/problem.

- We can end the activity with an additional similar problem for all students to complete quietly on their own. Students will hand in this last new problem like an exit slip. In addition, we might ask students what strategy they found most beneficial, or what their partner said that was most convincing.

WRITTEN ARGUMENTS

The more I use brief debate routines, from Soapbox Debates to Debate Cards, the more argumentation becomes a regular part of the classroom expectations. Students become accustomed to always providing an argument, even when I do not insist on one—music to this math teacher's ears!

Because I think creating arguments is so important for my young mathematicians, I now incorporate the claim and warrant Talking Routine into nearly everything I do in class, including written work. For instance, when creating some practice problems for the distance formula, I started a worksheet as shown in Figure 4.8. For your algebra class, you could have students work through a set of problems that started as shown in Figure 4.9.

For each of the problems below, decide the best way to solve for the distance between the given points-- Distance Formula or Pythagorean Theorem (by drawing in legs for a right triangle). Provide a warrant for your claim. Then solve the problem using what you think is the best method.

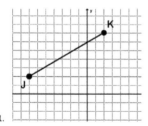

1.

2. Distance between (3, 24) and (-14, 33).

FIGURE 4.8

[58]

In each system of equations below, decide on the best method for solving the system (substitution, elimination, graphing). State your argument with a complete claim and warrant. Then solve the system.

1. $x + y = 11$
$3x - y = 5$

Claim: _____

Warrant: _____

_____

2. $y = x + 1$
$y = \frac{1}{2}x - 3$

Claim: _____

Warrant: _____

_____

FIGURE 4.9

We are all accustomed to completing math problems on paper. So why not make debate a part of this routine? As students work on problems in class or for homework, they can continue the habit of building arguments with the claim and warrant sentence starter. Written arguments are especially beneficial for quieter students because they give students the opportunities to practice preparing arguments without the pressure of verbalizing their ideas.

My students have come to expect that at least one question on every test or quiz will ask them to provide an argument. These problems can be as straightforward as the worksheet examples or more embedded in a real-world scenario like:

Mr. Luz is traveling abroad this summer and wants to get an international cell plan. Vertical Cellular will allow him to either:

Pay $45 for 100 minutes of calling.

Pay $1.10 per minute for any call.

Provide an argument as to which plan Mr. Luz should choose.

TEACHING PROOF

Whether or not I am teaching geometry, I believe creating warrants and developing students' argumentation is important. In addition, whenever I *do* teach a standard geometry class, one that includes formal proofs, it is often quite natural for my students to write proofs because of the debate routines. I start introducing these routines from the first week of school, and when we get to proofs—specifically two-column proofs—I just change the headings from "Statement" and "Reason" to "Claim" and "Warrant." Thus, a proof can look like Figure 4.10.

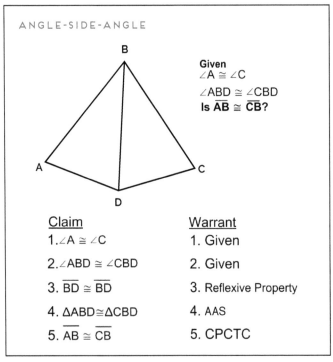

ANGLE-SIDE-ANGLE

Given
∠A ≅ ∠C
∠ABD ≅ ∠CBD
Is AB̄ ≅ C̄B̄?

Claim	Warrant
1. ∠A ≅ ∠C	1. Given
2. ∠ABD ≅ ∠CBD	2. Given
3. BD̄ ≅ BD̄	3. Reflexive Property
4. △ABD≅△CBD	4. AAS
5. AB̄ ≅ CB̄	5. CPCTC

FIGURE 4.10

Because students are accustomed to their answers in math class needing an explanation (a warrant), the two-column proof (or even a flowchart proof) makes sense to them. As one student said to me, "Well, obviously, you can't just say a bunch of facts. How will anyone understand why you won [the argument]?"

FALSIFICATION

What's My Rule? is an additional activity that can build a classroom culture of debate, and I often introduce it as a brief closing activity. It just takes about five minutes to get students developing arguments, and if we run out of time to complete it, all the better! Students will be talking about the problem and begging for the answer until next class.

Here is how it works. I start by putting a box on the board, as shown in Figure 4.11. Then, I slowly start adding some examples. Objects in the box adhere to my rule. Anything outside the box is a counterexample. So, I may first start by filling in a few numbers (Figure 4.12). Then, I ask students to guess my rule for allowing objects in the box. They must have a warrant for their guess. Often, at this early stage, I have students share their guesses/arguments with a neighbor, and I float around to hear what they are thinking. I may hear:

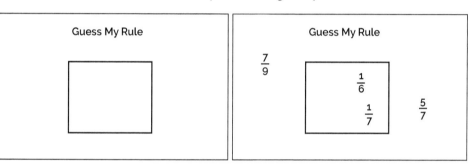

FIGURE 4.11   FIGURE 4.12

Judi: *I claim that the rule is only fractions with one in the numerator go in the box, and my warrant is the ones outside the box have bigger numbers.*

At this point, I know students have fallen for my trap. I was leading students down this (incorrect) path, seeing who would make quick assumptions. So, I ask students to see if their rule still holds when I add a few more examples (Figure 4.13).

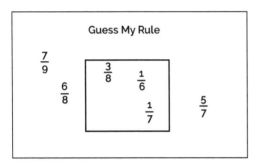

FIGURE 4.13

The point of this is to get my students thinking outside the box (pun in-tended!), looking at multiple options. In this particular example, I was looking at fractions less than one-half (in the box) versus those greater than one-half. However, part of the fun of this exercise is to watch students jump to conclusions. As students share out their guesses, I put in more evidence that falsifies their hypothesis, pushing them to reanalyze the information and create a new rule, based on updated evidence. My goal is for them to start with more general rules and work their way down to more specifics, as more examples appear.

THE END GOAL

As you can see, debate can take on many forms. We can play with debate in speaking or writing. We can encourage students to listen and respond to one another or take on an argument they may not originally side with. Debate and mathematical arguments can start to seep into all of our work in class. Feel free to play with these ideas and the variations shared, and even make your own!

Our goal is to create good habits of mind in our students around debate and argumentation. The more ways we reiterate the Talking Routine and the need for a strong warrant, the more we are infusing reasoning and explanation into our math classes. We want to raise all students' voices in the math classroom, especially students who have been historically excluded from or marginalized in mathematics. Our students have many opinions to share. They all want to critique the world around them, and our job is to help them find the words!

EXTRA TIME

One precalculus class, my principal stopped by for a quick observation. She had seen my students debate as a warm-up at least once before, and I was excited to "show off" for her again. We were in the middle of a unit that involved the law of sines and law of cosines, and students were debating: *What is the best tool for finding missing sides of triangles?* The class seemed to run smoothly.

The next day, my principal was not as giddy as I had expected. She said she was grateful that I was having students discuss in math class. However, she was wondering: What's next? Debate warm-ups and short debate activities had been a staple of my math classroom for a year or two at this point, and she was pushing me to go further with it. Could I have a goal beyond having students talk in math class? Could students dig deeper and debate math on a larger scale, tying in more real-world relevance?

Like many of us, my initial reaction to criticism was defensiveness. We all have those moments of frustration where an administrator (usually not a math teacher) gives us "advice" that is not what we expected to hear. I was frustrated. Yet, trying to be proactive, I decided to take her advice as a challenge. I would seek out or create larger activities for my students, ones grounded in real-world scenarios, that would involve students analyzing complex situations, perhaps as performance assessments.

LARGE DEBATE LOGISTICS

When the time came for me to attempt a larger debate, it was daunting. Like creating a new project for your class, full debate involved a lot more planning than a short warm-up activity. I was fortunate to have many wonderful friends and colleagues to brainstorm with, building on ideas from various resources. The first debate was a little rocky for me, but the students still enjoyed digging into the real-world context. Since that first attempt, I have learned a lot about facilitating larger debates, and here are general thoughts and details that have worked best:

1. A successful large-scale debate usually has two to four sides to it. Think of each side as a campaign, trying to convince the audience that their way is best. This variety of positions allows for multiple teams, each with different arguments to make.

2. Each team can have at least three and up to seven roles. There are three main roles, and I use extra roles to accommodate larger classes. No matter how many students per team, each student has a speaking role.

3. Preparation time for the students usually takes two or three full classes. Students spend one day working through the mathematics and then another day or two developing the team's arguments and speeches (although some of this could be assigned for homework too).

4. The debate itself takes an additional class day, usually between forty and fifty minutes. Teams participate in the whole-class debate and can be graded on their performances. Students can vote on the winning team, or we can invite adult or student volunteers to join the class and act as judges.

5. If you have a class smaller than twenty-eight, you can easily cut some of the roles (or cut one side of the debate). Scaling up for a larger group is a bit more complicated. Whenever you have a larger class, you could possibly (a) split the class in half and have two different debates ready, one for each half of the class or (b) have two or three of your students work on another assignment (perhaps catching up after missing some days of work) and then act as judges during the debate.

A SIMPLE SAMPLE

Before going into a large-scale math debate, let's look quickly at the flow of a medium one I developed a few years ago for a unit involving exponential functions and logarithms. Students should already have had some time to practice using logarithms to solve exponential equations before starting the debate, which usually takes three class days to prepare and execute.

On the first day of the debate work, students are introduced to the big question:

Which is a greater threat: outbreak or overpopulation?

Then, groups are given about twenty to thirty minutes to work on the following two problems.

1. Suppose a disease outbreak began with one case in December of last year. The disease then rapidly spread. By September, more than 8,000 cases were reported. If we let $x = 0$ represent last December (when there was only one case), can you create an exponential equation to model the number of cases?

2. The population of Earth is said to have reached two billion by 1927. Researching more data about the global population, can you create an exponential equation to model the population growth of humans on Earth?

This first day is mostly for understanding and modeling the information. Students are focused on the math, perhaps trying to create equations of the form $y = ae^{kx}$, and we can help support students as needed. Notice that the second question purposely only provides one data point. So, students will have to use additional resources to find more information about global population. Also, notice that students need to pay close attention to the different units being used (years versus months). As students finish their work, perhaps some groups can share out their equations and calculations. The goal for this first part of the work is to solidify an understanding of the computations.

Before the end of the first day, students should be assigned to one of two groups (either self-selected or your choice). One side will argue why overpopulation is the greatest threat to humanity, and the other side will argue that an uncontrolled disease outbreak is the greatest threat to humanity. Here is the debate prompt:

The United Nations has gathered a team to assess the greatest risk to humanity. The UN Ambassadors would like to set aside money to tackle one specific crisis. Where should they focus their attention? Below are the areas up for debate.

- Disease Outbreak—Will the next virus outbreak wipe out humanity? Looking at data from the spread of Ebola, we know that a disease could spread from 1 person to about 8,000 people in just nine months.
- Overpopulation—Will human overpopulation be the biggest crisis we face? Using projections on the population growth on Earth, we know there are already over seven billion people currently on the planet.

Which of these is the biggest concern for humanity?

This debate only has two sides. At the time I did this, I had about twenty-two students in the room. I split each side of the debate into two teams of five or six students. This meant that there were two groups arguing that disease outbreak is the biggest threat and two groups arguing that overpopulation is the biggest threat.

The second day of this activity is for preparing arguments. Students choose roles within their teams and prepare speeches or questions for the debate day. The basic roles include an opening speaker, a questioner, and a closing speaker, and pairs of students can work together on any of these roles. Students use this second day to draft their speeches, write questions, and get feedback from team members. The teams should work to have a cohesive set of warrants that they repeat throughout the debate. They should also list some weaknesses of the opposing team. Some of this work should involve outside research. In addition to the mathematical predictions, students should determine what other (perhaps nonmathematical) arguments are important. As the teacher, it is helpful to push the teams to think of multiple arguments.

The third day is the debate day. We may have other adults or students in the room to help judge. The debating students sit in their teams and the debate begins almost immediately. Because I had two teams for each side, we actually did the debate twice, with one outbreak team debating against one overpopulation team each time. Perhaps a larger class could do the debate three times, or another crisis could also be added for a third team to exist, but two teams for each side worked well. Here is the breakdown of the rounds:

- Round 1: Opening Speeches. One at a time, the opening speakers from each team stand up and give their opening speech. These speeches set the scene for the rest of the debate. This should take about two minutes per team.

  Team Outbreak: *Are you ready for the end of the world? It may be closer than you realize. One uncontrolled outbreak is all it would take to wipe out humanity. So this is the crisis that deserves all of your attention. We claim that an outbreak is the biggest threat to humanity, and we have three main warrants. First, a major outbreak could spread to the entire population in just two years. Second, without treatments, an outbreak is virtually unstoppable. Last, the costs to attempt to contain a major outbreak are higher than any other crisis. Only in funding prevention can we . . .*

- Round 2: Questioning. One team at a time, the questioner stands up and asks critical questions of the other team. This is the meat of the debate, where students verbally spar. The goal of the questions is to point out the weaknesses in the opposing side. The questioner asks one question at a time, and the team being asked has thirty seconds to respond. A specific student may be assigned the role of answerer, or the whole team can work together to respond to each question. Each team should be allowed about five minutes of questioning.

  Team Overpopulation: *To our Team Outbreak opponents—if countries with a spreading disease close their borders, doesn't that stop the spread and the threat to the global population?*

  Team Outbreak: *Any kind of border closure is only a temporary pause in the spread. Disease can spread by air or by water. There is no way to definitely stop the spread. It will still go up exponentially.*

  Team Overpopulation: *Furthermore, has your equation taken into account the large amount of rural areas, where spreading would slow down?*

- Round 3: Closing Speeches. One at a time, the closing speakers from each team stand up and give their final speech. These speeches wrap up the debate and should address any "weaknesses" brought out by other teams. Closing arguments should be limited to about two minutes per team.

Team Outbreak: I hope today we have convinced you that disease outbreak is the greatest threat to humanity. All of our time and money should be spent tackling this problem. We showed you just how quickly an uncontrolled outbreak can spread and wipe out humanity. Despite the other team's attempts to distract you with closing borders, airborne diseases will still spread and those closures are only temporary delays in the spread. Without a cure, the spread of disease is unstoppable. So, we should focus on prevention now. Overpopulation is a slow and controllable concern, while a disease outbreak is a fast-moving and expensive crisis. We must focus all of our energy on preventing and planning for the next outbreak.

I called this a medium debate, because, with only two teams and three rounds, it should only take about twenty to thirty minutes to complete in a class. With two teams for each side, I did the full debate twice, about twenty minutes each time. You can always shorten or lengthen the allowed time for each round based on your time constraints and goals for the activity. Also, students may not need the two full days to prepare for the debate. That is the planning I normally allow in a larger debate, but for a medium debate, students might be able to do the two days of preparation all in one.

A LONGER LESSON

With the outbreak/overpopulation example in mind, let us now explore a large-scale math debate:

A new but promising young artist is trying to decide how to produce her new record. Should she choose a major record label or a legitimate indie label? Are there other options? Below are her offers:

- Major Record Label—They want to sign the new artist. They will give the artist a $200,000 signing bonus, plus the artist will get $0.10 in royalty for each song sold.
- Indie Record Label—They want to sign the new artist. They offer a $50,000 signing bonus plus $0.60 in royalty for each song sold.
- Self-Employed Artists— who produce on their own get to keep all earnings. It will cost $20,000 for recording time and supplies, but once the record is made, the artist makes $0.80 per song sold.
- Eccentric Billionaire—A wealthy eccentric is interested in new business adventures. He offers the artist $300,000 for full rights to the songs. The billionaire keeps all earnings.

Assuming each song sells for $1.00 on iTunes, which team should our young musician choose?

This problem was lovingly adapted from the Boston Debate League.

This debate could serve as a performance assessment for an Algebra 1 unit on systems of equations. Similar to the outbreak/overpopulation example, different groups or teams will each be defending one of the options for the musician. For example, one group will argue that going with a major record label is the best option and provide several reasons why. Another team will be arguing that an independent record label is more reasonable and so on.

Because this is a larger debate, students usually need about three days to explore, research, and write out arguments for the debate. That is followed by a class day, not necessarily the next day, where students present their arguments in a full-scale debate. There is a lot to process for the students: the problem itself can take time to mathematically process, understanding the music industry can take some time (and research!), and writing compelling arguments based on all of the information is no easy task. So it is recommended to roll out the information slowly each day, giving students time to think, work, and process. What follows is my typical flow.

DAY 1—EXPLORING THE PROBLEM

The students usually need twenty or thirty minutes of class to explore the problem with their current partners. Students need this time to process the question, translate it to linear equations, and then solve the system to find the intersection points. Students should be doing the math for all four sides of the debate at this point. As a teacher, you need to be clear with students what tools they can use to solve this problem. Are you looking for algebraic work? Can students use graphing technology?

As you move around the room, listen carefully to student conversations. You can use this time to help those who are struggling with the concepts. Listen to how well students are able to identify the slope and y-intercept in this type of problem. Sometimes it is helpful to pause the class once or twice and have students share out some mathematical thinking they have done, correct or incorrect. It is not imperative that students have all correct work, but it is important that students have a solid understanding of the concepts and numerical relationships in this problem—this includes the meaning of the slopes, the y-intercepts, and the intersection points.

As students start to come up with intersection points (like $x = 350,000$ and $y = 260,000$), challenge them to first explain the meaning of these numbers (*Is that the amount of money they're making or . . . ?*). Then, ask if that number is plausible. How many songs does an average artist sell? What about a new musician? What seems reasonable? This line of questioning gets students primed to do research on the music industry. Most of us (myself included) have no idea what to estimate as the number of songs a musician sells. Perhaps students can start looking up information online about their favorite artists in class. Or perhaps that will be their homework for the night?

Thus, the first day is all about exploration. We want students to start to grasp and feel comfortable with both the mathematical concepts and the music industry connections. Time permitting, we could assign students into four teams, perhaps randomly, perhaps not. These are their debate teams. It is helpful to mix up the students at this point, so they are working with peers other than those partners they were just working with, enabling more sharing of ideas and a chance to compare mathematical precision. Based on our observations, we may also be ready to assign each group a side of the debate that they would be happy defending.

Day 2 is the student research day. On the day of the debate, teams will have to state their claims (e.g., "We claim self-employed is the best option for this new musician.") with at least three warrants. At least two of the warrants need to be grounded in mathematics (such as, "After 350,000 songs sold, our option is the most profitable, as you can see from our work."). Any other warrants can be more emotional ("Independent record labels will really care about you and devote time to you.") or based on facts about the music industry ("A major record label has many more connections and can keep you on an ever-increasing trajectory.").

In preparation for the full debate, the first goal for this day is for each team to come up with their three to five strongest warrants. Students explore both the mathematical and the real-world facts behind their side of the debate. They may need to do a lot of online research about the music industry. They need to find comfort discussing the differences between major record labels and independent record labels—differences I had to learn myself! As a team, they should decide on and rank their strongest reasons and start to outline what they want to say about each of these points. To monitor student work, we can have checkpoints, such as: "After twenty minutes of class, I want to see your list of the three to five most compelling warrants for your side of the debate." For any mathematical arguments, we can require students to explain the work behind their calculations.

We want students to spend the first half of class mainly focused on their assigned side of the debate. Then, once their team has compiled its list of most compelling arguments, they can spend the next part of class researching the other sides of the debate. Ask students to learn about the strengths of each of the other sides and discuss arguments to counter those strengths. For instance, ask: *If the eccentric billionaire earns the musician the most money up front, what will your team argue to counter that positive aspect?* This preparation will allow them to quickly respond to other teams during the debate. For students or classes that could use a bit of structure, the following chart can hold teams accountable, acting as the second checkpoint for the day (Table 5.1). (The part in italics is an example I added.)

TEAM	STRONG WARRANT	YOUR COUNTERARGUMENT
Self-employed	*Will make the most money after xxx songs sold*	*That is a huge* IF*! They start in the negative and have a large uphill climb to get connected and sold.*

TABLE 5.1

DAY 3—DEVELOPING ROLES

Day 3 day is when students start putting everything down into writing, getting ready to present for the debate in a following class. It is helpful to start this day by explaining the roles in the debate. Each group will have to determine who will take on which roles. The four main roles are listed in Table 5.2.

ROLE	DESCRIPTION
Opener	This student introduces the main arguments for their team's side of the debate. They must write a speech that catches the attention of the audience and convincingly explains the main warrants for that team's side of the debate. For any mathematical arguments, the math work must also be explained.
Questioner	This student asks questions to gently point out the weakness in the other sides of the debate. By asking questions of each of the other teams, this student will expose disadvantages to the other sides of the debate. This student must think quickly on their feet, as this person will also be responsible for defending their own side of the debate when answering the questions other questioners ask of their team.
Cross-examiner*	This student is responsible for making all the other teams look bad. In a brief speech, going team by team, this student will summarize any of the flaws that have already been mentioned and explain any additional disadvantages of each opposing side of the debate.
Closer	This student will have the final say for their team. This student must skillfully and engagingly summarize all the reasons their team is the best option and should adapt their speech based on points made during the earlier rounds of the debate.

For smaller groups, the cross-examiner role of the debate could be the first one cut.
TABLE 5.2

Some of these roles (like questioner and cross-examiner, or even the opener) could be shared between two students. So, if we need to have larger teams of seven or eight students (and I do not recommend having larger teams than that, if possible), have two students work together as questioners, cross-examiners, or perhaps as openers with a joint opening statement.

In addition, all teams should assign a team manager (Table 5.3). This person keeps everyone motivated and organized and also can step in for a student who is absent the day of the debate. This leader could be a separate role, or each team's manager may also have another role (like opener).

ROLE	DESCRIPTION
Team Manager	This student is responsible for the entire team. They should help all members of the team develop arguments, speeches, and questions. This student is the timekeeper for the group, making sure everyone completes work in a timely manner and reminding team members of any work that needs to be completed. Most important, this student should have copies of all work and speeches for all members of the team, as the team manager will be responsible for filling the roles of any team members who are absent on the day of the debate.

TABLE 5.3

Once roles are assigned, students get to work writing their speeches or questions. Students have the rest of the class period to write and practice their speeches, and they are more than welcome to continue to work on them and rehearse them at home. The questioner is the only role that does not involve writing a speech. Students who are taking on the role of questioner could be required to do the following:

1. List five to ten questions to ask *each* of the other teams. These questions should be focused to point out the other teams' weaknesses.

2. List ideas to defend the weakest points of their own team. Consider the questions other teams will use to critique their team, and make a bullet-point list of responses they will use to defend their team's weaknesses.

The role of the teacher at this point is to check in with each group, answer questions, and push students to strengthen their arguments. We can ask individual students to share some of their speech or questions and try to play devil's advocate, challenging their arguments. We want our students to think deeply about their reasoning and also be clear on their mathematical explanations.

One quick piece of advice I will mention here is to have groups make posters (or slides or something permanent) with all of their math work. During a debate, students tend to speak quickly. It can be hard to keep up with arguments and explanations. Also, each part of the debate will be timed, and students do not need to walk the class laboriously through each step of solving a system of equations. It will be hard to check any mathematical reasoning ("The intersection point is 350,000 because we set the equations equal to each other and got . . .") unless it is all prewritten on a poster that the speaker(s) can point to while quickly explaining their conclusions.

This third day of developing arguments or any of the previous days of work could also stretch over two days (if time permits). It is important to give students enough time to prepare both the mathematical and the real-world arguments. We want to have a great debate!

A quick note about grading: If we want to assign students points for their work, there are several options. First, during the work days, there could be exit slips or speech-writing goals, where students hand in their work for points. Additionally, I like to have students formatively assess one another within their groups. Written assessments (no points necessarily) could be really powerful here. Furthermore, as this as a performance task, we need a clear rubric for the students' performances on the day of the debate. Here is one possibility:

MATHEMATICAL DEBATE RUBRIC

START of Debate _____ / 5
Your team was ready to go at the start of the period by:
• being in your seat, **sitting quietly** at the bell
• having out all **notes** or speeches
• being ready to begin at the start of class

SPEAKING _____ / 15
You delivered your speech/questions appropriately by:
• speaking **clearly** and confidently
• having notes or questions **prepared** ahead of time
• **numbering** your main points
• **using evidence** in your explanation
  ○ citing all sources
  ○ showing all math

MATHEMATICAL DEBATE RUBRIC CONTINUED

LISTENING _____ / 15
You showed you were an excellent audience member by:
- **silently listening** to all other speakers
- sitting up, leaning in
- taking **notes** on each team's claims and rebuttals
- writing down notes to **help** your team's speakers

Note: any talking out of turn is −1 each time for your entire team.

WRAP-UP _____ / 5
You helped end the debate by:
- applauding everyone's hard work
- thoughtfully completing the exit slip/voting
- cleaning up all materials
- putting desks back in order

Once students have prepared their speeches and questions, they will be ready for the debate. The full-period debate could happen the very next day, or it could be further off. I find it helpful to schedule the debate a few days later in case students need more time to research and rehearse on their own time. We may move on with different material in class, but students have a few more evenings to write and practice their roles.

DAY 4—THE DEBATE PERFORMANCE

On the day of presentations, I like to invite a few teachers or administrators who are interested to come help us judge (if possible). They will listen to the arguments and cast votes. Students will also cast votes at the end as well. To keep from running out of time, we need to set the expectation that we will begin immediately at the start of class. The debate then moves through four rounds (Table 5.4):

ROUND	TIMING	DESCRIPTION
1 Opening Speeches	2–3 minutes/ team (8–12 minutes total)	Each of the four teams presents an opening speech, one at a time. All teams should be listening carefully to the arguments each team is starting with so they know what to attack!
2 Questioning	5 minutes/ team (20 minutes total)	Each of the four teams gets a chance to ask questions of the other teams. The first team has a questioner stand and ask questions of any of the other teams (addressing which team the question is directed to). After each question, the team asked has a chance to respond briefly. After the 5 minutes are up, the next team's questioner stands and asks the questions, listening to the answers from each team. This continues until all four teams have had their chance to ask questions.
3 Cross-Examining	2 minutes/ team (8 minutes total)	Each of the four teams presents a cross-examination speech, one at a time. These are direct attacks that should directly address any of the points the other teams consider as strengths, pointing out weakness in other teams. All teams should be listening carefully to what is said about their own team. It is the job of the closer to counter these charges at the end.
4 Closing	2 minutes/ team (8 minutes total)	Similar to the opening speech round, each of the four teams presents a closing speech, one at a time. This is each team's final word on why they should win the debate!

TABLE 5.4

Here are a few tips and ideas for running this full-scale debate:

- A team's arguments should be rooted in the math. Make sure this expectation is clear to openers and questioners especially.

- Often, the opening speeches are two minutes or less. If they run a bit short, use the extra time for the questioning round, as it can take the longest. (You could also cut time by shortening the questioning round to three or four minutes, if needed.)

- The questioning round can be most difficult to facilitate because there is some back-and-forth between teams (a question asked then answered). You may need to remind students to be brief in their replies, perhaps giving time warnings.

- To keep things focused, we can assign each questioner only one team to question (way ahead of time in the planning stages). For instance, the major record label team will only question the indie record label team. And the indie record label team will only question the self-employed team, and so on.

- If you have a smaller group, the cross-examining round can be eliminated. The closing speaker can cross-examine while summarizing.

- According to the rubric, each person on the team loses a point when someone is talking out of turn. This helps keep it to only one person speaking at a time. However, students are *highly* encouraged to pass notes during the debate to share ideas with one another during the debate. The closer will appreciate helpful notes of what to add in the final speech.

- Grading with the rubric can be tough while students are talking. You will need one rubric per group. Have all four sitting out in front of you so you can jot quick notes. Then, go back and fill out one sheet per student later that day. Alternatively, you could video record the debate to look back on later.

FINAL REFLECTIONS

At the end of the debate, have students fill out a brief exit slip where they reflect on their performance and vote for the winners. I like to ask:

1. What are you most proud of in this debate?
2. What do you wish you could improve on for the next debate?
3. Which two teams were the most convincing in this debate? (One of these teams can be your own!)

It is important that students take time to thoughtfully reflect on the debate. Their thoughts immediately following the debate can be referred to the next time you are preparing students for a debate, and they can help you work through what you want to keep or change before doing a similar activity again.

I have found full-scale debates to be great replacements for projects, tests, posters, or other displays of work because they are so *alive*. Students are excited to work on the mathematics and research the context. They are eager to share their opinions and debate with their classmates. And, for the teacher, it is often more exciting to furiously grade a debate happening during the class period than to bring a bunch of projects home to grade one by one.

What's more, these summative debates have led many students to say that they *finally* see math as relevant. Despite our constant attempts to show students how the topics they study could be used in the real world, year after year, students have said that the debates are where they really saw math as a tool to help understand the real world.

CHAPTER 6

CLOSING ARGUMENTS

n the wake of the school shooting at Marjory Stoneman Douglas High School in Parkland, Florida, in February 2018, the debate about gun control returned to center stage. No matter what side of the debate you are on, the confidence and poise with which some of the surviving students spoke out in the weeks and months following the tragedy was noteworthy. According to their superintendent, "What really explains the students' poise . . . is the school district's system-wide debate program that teaches extemporaneous speaking from an early age" (Gurney 2018). The students of Marjory Stoneman Douglas High School had the option of debate as both an extracurricular activity and a course during the school day. By practicing forming arguments—prepared or impromptu—students learned to speak up and speak out with calm and informed professionalism. That is the power of debate. It provides a space for multiple perspectives, and it honors students' voices.

Now, imagine all the ways we can raise our students' voices if we add frequent debate to math lessons. Building routines for formal discourse can help students learn to speak up in productive ways. Students can disagree civilly. With the rise of social media and the divisiveness in our current political climate, I feel compelled to help students find ways to constructively critique the reasoning of others. This is why debate in math class is so important. We are raising the next generation of adults, and we cannot ignore character growth in math class. Good discourse can be embedded in the lesson, not a stand-alone event.

What's more, as a *New York Times* opinion article by University of Pennsylvania's Adam Grant quipped, "If kids never get exposed to disagreement, we'll end up limiting their creativity" (2017). Students' opinions and personalities are important and should be valued in inclusive classrooms. Math class is no exception. We want students to know that anyone can talk and debate, including with mathematics. We want them to know that math can involve opinions, and we want them to feel that math can be simultaneously controversial and beautiful.

Mathematics is a subject solidly grounded in reasoning and proof, so argumentation should be a core part of the math classroom. These arguments also bring focus onto the mathematical process. By debating, we are helping our students see math class as a place where reasoning, understanding, and interpretation are more important than answer-getting. Debate routines allow students to shift their mindset from the idea that math is where you learn a new formula and solve worksheet problems to the idea math is a living subject, where people discuss and debate best strategies or interpretations of information.

YOUR TEACHER TEAM

The Talking Routine of "My claim is . . . , and my warrant is . . ." is the heart of all the activities we have explored in this book. Formalizing students' language and focusing arguments on the best or the coolest example heightens the discourse and can deepen student understanding. The seeds for all of these ideas were planted by the National Speech & Debate Association (NSDA), a national organization that works to empower students through speech and debate competitions. As a student member when I was in high school, I learned invaluable skills for discussing and debating ideas. I continued learning from the NSDA as an adult and debate coach. If you want to find more resources for growing debate activities for your classroom (or want to expand into a competitive speech and debate team!), explore their website for more information. Like the students at Marjory Stoneman Douglas High School, your students can be empowered by this organization. Find out more at www.speechanddebate.org.

Jumping into debate can seem daunting at first, but I encourage you to start simple. Start by focusing on the routine. Warrants do not have to be stellar the first or second (or tenth) time you debate. Just know that they will improve, with practice and your guidance.

And know that you are not alone. It can easily feel overwhelming to start something new, but you have help. Plenty of teachers have started debating in math class, and they gladly share their ideas. I mentioned #DebateMath a few times in this book. If you are on Twitter (and if you aren't, get on it!), search for that hashtag to see some of what others have shared—both in exemplary problems you can use and in anecdotes of attempts with students. Know that plenty of teachers in the online community will happily support you. All you have to do is speak up!

Let me introduce you to a few of the teachers I have met that help, support, and inspire me. We are a team.

THE CASE OF KARLA

One of the first teachers to invite me into her classroom after hearing these debate ideas was Karla Doyle (@mathwithdoyle). Karla is a math teacher, instructional leader, and mother living in Huntington Beach, California. She is a veteran teacher and a lifelong learner. She was still new to debating in math class when I had the opportunity to visit her middle school classroom.

I remember how nervous Karla was when I visited. She had prepared Debate Cards for students to practice simplifying expressions (see Figure 6.1) that she handed out to each pair. In addition, she created a handout where students could record their work and their arguments (see Figure 6.2).

Karla was nervous, but her students were not. Just moments after passing out the cards, students were engaged in discussing methods for simplifying the expressions and debating the best method. The room came alive quickly with rich discourse about the mathematical content. Students were having so much fun debating in math class that after completing the given work, pairs of students made videos of themselves debating a chosen problem that they shared with their teacher. What an exciting moment for Karla!

I recently asked Karla to summarize her thoughts on debate routines in math class. The first thing she said to me was, "I love debating in math class!" She went on to say:

> From my experience, I have found it engages the students and gets them
> talking math! I especially love the language of "My claim is . . . My
> warrant is . . ." My students have responded to that more than "show your
> work." I truly think it makes them all feel like mathematicians both in

A

Combining like terms is the first best step.

$$5x + 3x - 8 = 16$$

B

Adding 8 is the first best step.

A

Combining the like terms without the variables is the best first step.

$$\frac{2}{5}y + 4 + 7 + \frac{9}{10}y$$

B

Finding common denominators for the fractions and combining those terms is the first best step.

A

Subtracting four is the first best step.

$$2(n + 2) + 4 = 12$$

B

Distributing 2 is the fist best step.

FIGURE 6.1

	Name ______________________
Circle: A or B	
Solve. $5x + 3x - 8 = 16$	My claim is ____________________ ____________________ ____________________ ____________________. My warrant is ____________________ ____________________ ____________________ ____________________ ____________________ ____________________ ____________________ ____________________.
Simplify. $\frac{2}{5}y + 4 + 7 + \frac{9}{10}y$	My claim is ____________________ ____________________ ____________________ ____________________. My warrant is ____________________ ____________________ ____________________ ____________________ ____________________ ____________________ ____________________ ____________________.

FIGURE 6.2

dialogue and while doing traditional paper/pencil work . . . I have seen my students feel more passionate about what they are learning. They want to defend their work and challenge others. It is awesome!

Her advice to all of you out there was to not be afraid to try. Focus on the good in each attempt.

PATRICIA'S PRACTICUM

Another California teacher that wowed me was Patricia Vandenberg (@Vberg-Math). She learned about debating math ideas at a conference one weekend and jumped right into implementing it that following Monday morning. Her tweet that Monday included the photo in Figure 6.3.

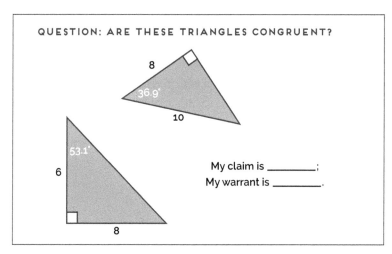

QUESTION: ARE THESE TRIANGLES CONGRUENT?

8
36.9°
10
53.1°
6
8

My claim is _____;
My warrant is _____.

FIGURE 6.3

Patricia is a high school math teacher who, as of this writing, teaches Integrated Math 1 and 2. She is a wonderful teacher whose goal is to help her students see the beauty in mathematics. Though she was quick to jump in with these routines, she would say you don't have to rush. She tells teachers: "Don't be afraid to start small; be brave and go for it because it will transform the math discussions in your classroom."

I particularly loved one of Patricia's reactions during her first few days debating math. She said: "The students who were speaking/arguing most today were the ones that speak the least on most days." Through her guidance and facilitation, Patricia saw the power of these speaking routines. All students felt invited to the discussion. All students could engage in math class.

Patricia went on to say:

The way we teach math has changed and the learning goals for students have evolved past just knowing how to do something and now include why. I've noticed students really struggle with articulating the why . . . So often they say something like "I just did it in my head!" Or "I don't know, it just is that way." Including debate math [routines] in my lessons has given students a way to explain themselves in a clear, safe, and structured format. The [Talking Routines] . . . make students elevate their own language, and I find my students' explanations are much clearer and centered around solid math concepts, instead of what they just feel or assume.

CLAIRE'S CONVERSATION

Claire Verti (@ClaireVerti) works with Patricia Vandenberg in La Verne, California. She has taught high school math for the past sixteen years and has just started debating in math class. When I met with her, she said: "I introduced my students to debate [routines] . . . about a month ago. Immediately, I found that the [Talking Routines] helped my students create much better mathematical arguments . . . Since introducing debate math to my classroom, I've noticed that situations pop up almost every day that I can use debate." She excitedly wrote me the following story:

Today was the second day back from spring break. My students were using the remainder theorem and polynomial division to write a polynomial function with a not equal to 1 in factored form. There was a point that they had the quadratic seen in Figure 6.4.

$$6x^2 + x - 1$$

FIGURE 6.4

The students were working in teams on whiteboards so I could see that they were realizing that their answers were different from their neighbors and there was a buzz about which answer was correct. So I pulled the class together, saying that I'd seen three different answers. I wrote them on the board (Figure 6.5), and I asked them to come up with an argument for which one is correct. I gave them a minute to think and discuss.

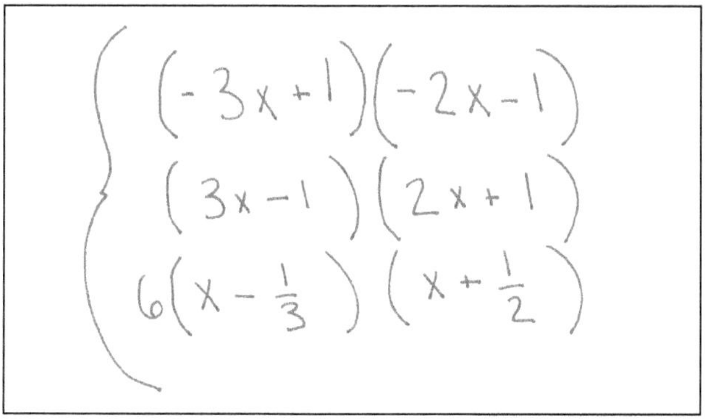

$$\left\{ \begin{array}{l} (-3x+1)(-2x-1) \\ (3x-1)(2x+1) \\ 6\left(x-\frac{1}{3}\right)\left(x+\frac{1}{2}\right) \end{array} \right.$$

FIGURE 6.5

Student 1: *My claim is that the third one is correct. My warrant is that I used the quadratic formula to find the roots of $\frac{1}{3}$ and $-\frac{1}{2}$ and wrote it in factored form with the a-value of 6 in the front.*

Student 2: *My claim is that none of them are correct. My warrant is that I didn't get those answers.*

The class erupted in laughter as the student grinned.

Student 3: *My claim is that the second one is correct. My warrant is that I factored it with the area model and the x-box and that's my answer.*

Then I told my students to graph all four expressions to find out which one is correct. The students grumbled when it turned out they were all *correct.*

Student 4: *I had a feeling you were trying to trick us.*

Teacher: *Since all three are equivalent to the quadratic expression, I want to know which one you think is most correct.*

They talked for a minute in their teams.

Student 5: *My claim is that the second one is most correct. My warrant is that there are no fractions and the coefficients of x are not negative.*

Student 6: *My claim is that the third one is correct. My warrant is that when you look at the binomials you can already see the roots are $\frac{1}{3}$ and $-\frac{1}{2}$ without having to do any math in your head.*

Then I asked for someone to restate these last two arguments.

> **Student 7:** *Student 5's claim was that the second one was correct. Their warrant was that there were no fractions or negatives in front of the x's.*

> **Student 8:** *Student 6's claim is that the third one is correct. Their warrant is that when you use the zero product property and set it equal to solve for the roots, you only need to add and subtract. Whereas with the other ones, you have to add or subtract and then multiply. That's two things.*

I really enjoyed reading her script of what happened for several reasons. First, I enjoyed the recount of how Claire led a debate routine in the moment. She had set up the routine enough times (in just a few weeks) that students were able to jump right into it. Additionally, I like that she allowed a student (Student 2) to make a nonmathematical statement ("I didn't get those answers"). Not only did that student feel safe enough to share out that he or she had a different answer, but it shows that not all students have to be sharing stellar statements at all times. Some of these moments, especially ones that are happening on the fly, can be messy at times, and that is OK.

Throughout the debate, we should also note the think time allowed. As she asked the question and later changed the question, Claire gave students a chance to talk in their groups to process each question and practice what they want to say. Last, by adding a second layer to the debate (Which answer is most correct?), she was able hear more of her students' thinking, and more importantly, they were able to hear ideas from one another. As Claire says, "Your students will often surprise you in how they think about mathematics and how they justify their answer. It had not occurred to me to say the third one was most correct, but after hearing the students' arguments, I think I changed my mind."

If you talk with Claire, you will hear her say how much she loves to debate math because it's a simple strategy that "can be used almost every day to yield high impact in a student's ability to reason and justify their statements." Her advice is to "Just try it." What is the worst that can happen? The lesson might fail, and you try something else the next day. But it could also be amazing.

MY FINAL PLEA

I hope the ideas and examples in this book have been helpful to you. I hope you can see many possibilities for your class. This work is for you to take and make your own. We all want to inspire students to reach their potential and improve the world around them, and we can do that in math class!

For more examples, videos, and ideas, visit luzniak.com. Specific examples to go with this book can be found at luzniak.com/debatebook. We are constantly growing the examples and resources on the website. Feel free to browse anytime or submit your own examples.

Last, please help grow the community. Add more resources. Share your awesome ideas on social media using @cluzniak or using the hashtag #DebateMath. Share the information. Let's help change math class into a place where debate is the norm. Let's help create future mathematicians who know how to create viable arguments and critique the reasoning of others.

REFERENCES

Bellon, Joe. 2000. "A Research-Based Justification for Debate Across the Curriculum." *Argumentation and Advocacy* 36 (3): 161–175.

Carpenter, Thomas P., Megan Loef Franke, and Linda Levi. 2003. *Thinking Mathematically: Integrating Arithmetic & Algebra in Elementary School.* Portsmouth, NH: Heinemann.

Common Core, National Governors Association Center for Best Practices, Council of Chief State School Officers. 2010. Common Core State Standards (Mathematics). Washington, DC: National Governors Association Center for Best Practices, Council of Chief State School Officers.

Danielson, Christopher. 2016. *Which One Doesn't Belong? A Shapes Book.* Portland, ME: Stenhouse.

Grant, Adam. "Kids, Would You Please Start Fighting?" *New York Times,* November 4, 2017. https://www.nytimes.com/2017/11/04/opinion /sunday/kids-would-you-please-start-fighting.html?smid=tw-share.

Gurney, Kyra. 2018. "Last Fall, They Debated Gun Control in Class. Now, They Debate Lawmakers on TV." *Miami Herald*, February 23. https://www. miamiherald.com/news/local/education/article201678544.html.

Horn, Ilana Seidel. 2017. *Motivated: Designing Math Classrooms Where Students Want to Join In.* Portsmouth, NH: Heinemann.

Kazemi, Elham, and Allison Hintz. 2014. *Intentional Talk: How to Structure and Lead Productive Mathematical Discussions.* Portland, ME: Stenhouse.

Liljedahl, Peter. 2014. "The Affordances of Using Visually Random Groups in a Mathematics Classroom." In *Transforming Mathematics Instruction: Multiple Approaches and Practices*, ed. Y. Li, E. Silver, and S. Li. New York: Springer.

Mercer, Neil, and Steve Hodgkinson. 2008. *Exploring Talk in Schools.* London: Sage.

National Council of Teachers of Mathematics. 2014. *Principles to Actions: Ensuring Mathematical Success for All.* Reston, VA: NCTM.

PBS Learning Media. n.d. "Encouraging Debate." PBS video, 4:54. https://witf. pbslearningmedia.org/resource/mtc13.pd.math.deb/encouraging-debate/.

Stanislavski, Constantin. 1936. *An Actor Prepares.* New York: Theater Arts.

INDEX